ELAINE SCARRY

On Beauty

AND

BEING JUST

PRINCETON UNIVERSITY
PRESS
PRINCETON AND OXFORD

Delivered as a Tanner Lecture on Human Values
at Yale University, 1998. Printed with permission of the
Tanner Lectures on Human Values, a
Corporation, University of Utah, Salt Lake City, Utah.

Fifth printing, and first paperback printing, 2001
Paperback ISBN 0-691-08959-0

The Library of Congress has cataloged the cloth edition of this book as follows

Scarry, Elaine
On beauty and being just / Elaine Scarry.
p.   cm.
Includes bibliographical references.
ISBN 0-691-04875-4 (cloth : alk. paper)
1. Aesthetics.   1. Title.
BH39 .S322   1999
111'.85—dc21   99-35075

This book has been composed in Monotype Centaur
by Gretchen Oberfranc *and* designed by Jan Lilly

Printed on acid-free paper. ∞

www.pup.princeton.edu

Printed in the United States of America

25   27   29   30   28   26

ISBN-13: 978-0-691-08959-1

ISBN-10: 0-691-08959-0

for Philip Fisher

CONTENTS

∽

PART ONE

On Beauty and
Being Wrong

WHAT IS THE felt experience of cognition at the moment one stands in the presence of a beautiful boy or flower or bird? It seems to incite, even to require, the act of replication. Wittgenstein says that when the eye sees something beautiful, the hand wants to draw it.

Beauty brings copies of itself into being. It makes us draw it, take photographs of it, or describe it to other people. Sometimes it gives rise to exact replication and other times to resemblances and still other times to things whose connection to the original site of inspiration is unrecognizable. A beautiful face drawn by Verrocchio suddenly glides into the perceptual field of a young boy named Leonardo. The boy copies the face, then copies the face again. Then again and again and again. He does the same thing when a beautiful living plant—a violet, a wild rose—glides into his field of vision, or a living face: he makes a first copy, a second copy, a third, a fourth, a fifth. He draws it over and over, just as Pater (who tells us all this about Leonardo) replicates—now in sentences—Leonardo's acts, so that the essay reenacts its subject, becoming a sequence of faces: an angel, a Medusa, a woman and child, a Madonna, John the Baptist, St. Anne, La Gioconda. Before long the means are found to replicate, thousands of times over, both the sentences and the faces, so that traces of Pater's paragraphs and Leonardo's drawings inhabit all the pockets of the world (as pieces of them float in the paragraph now before you).

A visual event may reproduce itself in the realm of touch (as when the seen face incites an ache of longing in the hand, and the hand then presses pencil to paper), which may in turn then reappear in a second visual event, the finished drawing. This crisscrossing of the senses may happen in any direction. Wittgenstein speaks not only about beautiful visual events prompting motions in the hand but, elsewhere, about heard music that later prompts a ghostly subanatomical event in his teeth and gums. So, too, an act of touch may reproduce itself as an acoustical event or even an abstract idea, the way whenever Augustine touches something smooth, he begins to think of music and of God.

Beauty Prompts a Copy of Itself

The generation is unceasing. Beauty, as both Plato's *Symposium* and everyday life confirm, prompts the begetting of children: when the eye sees someone beautiful, the whole body wants to reproduce the person. But it also—as Diotima tells Socrates—prompts the begetting of poems and laws, the works of Homer,

Hesiod, and Lycurgus. The poem and the law may then prompt descriptions of themselves—literary and legal commentaries—that seek to make the beauty of the prior thing more evident, to make, in other words, the poem's or law's "clear discernibility" even more "clearly discernible." Thus the beauty of Beatrice in *La vita nuova* requires of Dante the writing of a sonnet, and the writing of that one sonnet prompts the writing of another: "After completing this last sonnet I was moved by a desire to write more poetry." The sonnets, in turn, place on Dante a new pressure, for as soon as his ear hears what he has made in meter, his hand wants to draw a sketch of it in prose: "This sonnet is divided into two parts ..."; "This sonnet is divided into four parts. ..."[1]

This phenomenon of unceasing begetting sponsors in people like Plato, Aquinas, Dante the idea of eternity, the perpetual duplicating of a moment that never stops. But it also sponsors the idea of terrestrial plenitude and distribution, the will to make "more and more" so that there will eventually be "enough." Although very great cultural outcomes such as the *Iliad* or the *Mona Lisa* or the idea of distribution arise out of the requirement beauty places on us to replicate, the simplest manifestation of the phenomenon is the everyday fact of staring. The first flash of the bird incites the desire to duplicate not by translating the glimpsed image into a drawing or a poem or a photograph but simply by continuing to see her five seconds, twenty-five seconds, forty-five seconds later—as long as the bird is there to be beheld. People follow the paths of migrating birds, moving strangers, and lost manuscripts, trying to keep the thing sensorily present to them. Pater tells us that Leonardo, as though half-crazed, used to follow people around the streets of Florence once he got "glimpses of it [beauty] in the strange eyes or hair of chance people." Sometimes he persisted until sundown. This replication in the realm of sensation can be carried out by a single perceiver across time (one person staring at a face or listening to the unceasing song of a mockingbird) or can instead entail a brief act of perception distributed across many people. When Leonardo drew a cartoon of St. Anne, for "two days a crowd of people of all qualities passed in naive excitement through the chamber where it hung." This impulse toward a distribution across perceivers is, as both museums and postcards verify, the most common response to beauty: "Addis is full of blossoms. Wish you were here." "The nightingale sang again last night. Come here as soon as you can."

Beauty is sometimes disparaged on the ground that it causes a contagion of imitation, as when a legion of people begin to style themselves after a particular movie starlet, but this is just an imperfect version of a deeply beneficent momentum toward replication. Again beauty is sometimes disparaged because it gives rise to material cupidity and possessiveness; but here, too, we may come to feel we are simply encountering an imperfect instance of an otherwise positive outcome. If someone wishes all the Gallé vases of the world to sit on his own windowsills, it is just a miseducated version of the typically generous-hearted impulse we see when Proust stares at the face of the girl serving milk at a train stop:

> I could not take my eyes from her face which grew larger as she approached, like a sun which it was somehow possible to stare at and which was coming nearer and nearer, letting itself be seen at close quarters, dazzling you with its blaze of red and gold.[2]

Proust wishes her to remain forever in his perceptual field and will alter his own location to bring that about: "to go with her to the stream, to the cow, to the train, to be always at her side."

This willingness continually to revise one's own location in order to place oneself in the path of beauty is the basic impulse underlying education. One submits oneself to other minds (teachers) in order to increase the chance that one will be looking in the right direction when a comet makes its sweep through a certain patch of sky. The arts and sciences, like Plato's dialogues, have at their center the drive to confer greater clarity on what already has clear discernibility, as well as to confer initial clarity on what originally has none. They are a key mechanism in what Diotima called begetting and what Tocqueville called distribution. By perpetuating beauty, institutions of education help incite the will toward continual creation. Sometimes their institutional gravity and awkwardness can seem tonally out of register with beauty, which, like a small bird, has an aura of fragility, as when Simone Weil in *Waiting for God* writes:

> The love of the beauty of the world . . . involves . . . the love of all the truly precious things that bad fortune can destroy. The truly precious things are those forming ladders reaching toward the beauty of the world, openings onto it.

But Weil's list of precious things, openings into the world, begins not with a flight of a bird but with education: "Numbered among them are the pure and authentic achievements of art and sciences."[3] To misstate, or even merely understate, the relation of the universities to beauty is one kind of error that can be made. A university is among the precious things that can be destroyed.

Errors in Beauty:
Attributes Evenly and Unevenly Present
across Beautiful Things

The author of the *Greater Hippias*, widely believed to have been Plato, points out that while we know with relative ease what a beautiful horse or a beautiful man or possibly even a beautiful pot is (this last one is a matter of some dispute in the dialogue), it is much more difficult to say what "Beauty" un-attached to any object is. At no point will there be any aspiration to speak in these pages of unattached Beauty, or of the attributes of unattached Beauty. But there are attributes that are, without exception, present across different objects (faces, flowers, bird-songs, men, horses, pots, and poems), one of which is this impulse toward begetting. It is impossible to conceive of a beautiful thing that does not have this attribute. The homely word "replication" has been used here because it reminds us that the benign im-pulse toward creation results not just in famous paintings but in everyday acts of staring; it also re-minds us that the generative object continues, in some sense, to be present in the newly begotten ob-ject. It may be startling to speak of the *Divine Comedy* or the *Mona Lisa* as "a replication" since they are so unprecedented, but the word recalls the fact that something, or someone, gave rise to their creation and remains silently present in the newborn object.

In the case just looked at, then, the attribute was one common across all sites, and the error, when it briefly arose, involved seeing an imperfect version of the attribute (imitation of starlets or, more seriously, material greed) and correctly spotting the association with beauty, but failing to recognize the thousands of good outcomes of which this is a deteriorated version. Rejecting the imperfect version of the phenomenon of begetting makes sense; what does not make sense is rejecting the general impulse toward begetting, or rejecting the beautiful things for giving rise to false, as well as true, versions of begetting. To disparage beauty for the sake not of one of its attributes but simply for a misguided version of one of its otherwise beneficent attributes is a common error made about beauty.

But we will also see that many errors made about beauty arise not in relation to an attribute that is, without exception, common across all sites, but precisely in relation to attributes that are site-specific—that come up, for example, in relation to a beautiful garden but not in relation, say, to a beautiful poem; or come up in relation to beautiful persons but not in relation to the beauty of gods. The discontinuities across sites are the source of many confusions, one of which will be looked at in detail in Part Two. But the most familiar encounter with error occurs within any one site.

Errors within Any One Site

It seems a strange feature of intellectual life that if you question people—"What is an instance of an intellectual error you have made in your life?"—no answer seems to come readily to mind. Somewhat better luck is achieved if you ask people (friends, students) to describe an error they have made about beauty. It may be helpful if, before proceeding, the reader stops and recalls—in as much detail as possible—an error he or she has made so that another instance can be placed on the page in conjunction with the few about to be described. It may be useful to record the error, or the revision, in as much detail as is possible because I want to make claims here about the way an error presents itself to the mind, and the accuracy of what I say needs alternative instances to be tested against. The error may be a misunderstanding in the reading of Schiller's "Ninth Letter" in his *Aesthetic Education of Man,* or a misreading of page eleven in Kant's *Third Critique.* But the question is more directly aimed at errors, and revisions, that have arisen in day-to-day life. In my own case, for example, I had ruled out palm trees as objects of beauty and then one day discovered I had made a mistake.

∽

Those who remember making an error about beauty usually also recall the exact second when they first realized they had made an error. The revisionary moment comes as a perceptual slap or slam that itself has emphatic sensory properties. Emily Dickinson's poem—

> It dropped so low—in my Regard—
> I heard it hit the Ground—

is an instance. A correction in perception takes place as an abrasive crash. Though it has the sound of breaking plates, what is shattering loudly is the perception itself:

> It dropped so low—in my Regard—
> I heard it hit the Ground—
> And go to pieces on the Stones
> At bottom of my mind—[4]

The concussion is not just acoustic but kinesthetic. Her own brain is the floor against which the felt impact takes place.

The same is true of Shakespeare's "Lilies that fester smell far worse than weeds." The correction, the alteration in the perception, is so palpable that it is as though the perception itself (rather than its object) lies rotting in the brain. In both cases, the perception has undergone a radical alteration—it breaks apart (as in breaking plates) or disintegrates (as in the festering flower); and in both cases, the alteration is announced by a striking sensory event, a loud sound, an awful smell. Even if the alteration in perception were registered not as the sudden introduction of a negative sensation but as the disappearance of the positive sensory attributes the thing had when it was beautiful, the moment might be equally stark and highly etched. Gerard Manley Hopkins confides calmly, cruelly, to someone he once loved that his love has now almost disappeared. He offers as a final clarifying analogy what happens when a poem, once held to be beautiful, ceases to be so:

> Is this made plain? What have I come across
> That here will serve me for comparison?
> The sceptic disappointment and the loss
> A boy feels when the poet he pores upon
> Grows less and less sweet to him, and
> knows no cause.

No loud sound or bad smell could make this more devastating. But why? In part, because what is so positive is here being taken away: sweet is a taste, a

smell, a sound—the word, of all words, closest to the
fresh and easy call of a bird; and conveying a be-
lovedness, an acuity of regard, as effortless and un-
asked-for as honeysuckle or sweet william. Fading
(one might hope) could conceivably take place as a
merciful numbing, a dulling, of perception, or a
turning away to other objects of attention. But the
shades of fading here take place under the scrutiny of
bright consciousness, the mind registering in techni-
color each successive nuance of its own bereavement.
Hopkins's boy, with full acuity, leans into, pores
upon, the lesson and the lessening.

Those who recall making an error in beauty inevitably describe one of two genres of mistake. The
first, as in the lines by Dickinson, Shakespeare, and
Hopkins, is the recognition that something formerly
held to be beautiful no longer deserves to be so regarded. The second is the sudden recognition that
something from which the attribution of beauty had
been withheld deserved all along to be so denomi-
nated. Of these two genres of error, the second seems
more grave: in the first (the error of overcrediting),
the mistake occurs on the side of perceptual generosity, in the second (the error of undercrediting) on
the side of a failed generosity. Doubting the severity
of the first genre of error does not entail calling into
question the pain the person feels in discovering her

mistake: she has lost the beautiful object in the same way as if it had remained beautiful but had suddenly moved out of her reach, leaving her stranded, betrayed; in actuality, the faithful object has remained within reach but with the subtraction of all attributes that would ignite the desire to lay hold of it. By either path the desirable object has vanished, leaving the brain bereft.

The uncompromising way in which errors in beauty make themselves felt is equally visible in the second, more severe genre of intellectual error, where something not regarded as beautiful suddenly alerts you to your error. A better description of the moment of instruction might be to say—"Something you did not hold to be beautiful suddenly turns up in your arms arrayed in full beauty"—because the force and pressure of the revision is exactly as though it is happening one-quarter inch from your eyes. One lets things into one's midst without accurately calculating the degree of consciousness required by them. It is as though, when you were about to walk out onto a ledge, you had contracted to carry something, and only once out on the precipice did you realize that the object weighed one hundred pounds.

How one walks through the world, the endless small adjustments of balance, is affected by the shifting weights of beautiful things. Here the alternatives

posed a moment ago about the first genre of error—
where the beautiful object vanished, not because the
still-beloved object itself disappeared carrying its
beauty with it, but because the object stayed behind
with its beauty newly gone—are reversed. In the second genre of error a beautiful object is suddenly
present, not because a new object has entered the
sensory horizon bringing its beauty with it (as when
a new poem is written or a new student arrives or a
willow tree, unleafed by winter, becomes electric—a
maze of yellow wands lifting against lavender clap-
boards and skies) but because an object, already
within the horizon, has its beauty, like late luggage,
suddenly placed in your hands. This second genre of
error entails neither the arrival of a new beautiful
object, nor an object present but previously un-
noticed, but an object present and confidently repudiated as an object of beauty.

My palm tree is an example. Suddenly I am on a
balcony and its huge swaying leaves are before me at
eye level, arcing, arching, waving, cresting and breaking in the soft air, throwing the yellow sunlight up
over itself and catching it on the other side, running
its fingers down its own piano keys, then running them back up again, shuffling and dealing glit-
tering decks of aqua, green, yellow, and white. It is
everything I have always loved, fernlike, featherlike,
fanlike, open—lustrously in love with air and light.

The vividness of the palm states the acuity with which I feel the error, a kind of dread conveyed by the words "How many?" How many other errors lie like broken plates or flowers on the floor of my mind? I pore over the floor but cannot see much surface since all the space is taken up by the fallen tree trunk, the big clumsy thing with all its leaves stuffed into one shaft. But there may be other things down under there. When you make an error in beauty, it should set off small alarms and warning lights. Instead it waits until you are standing on a balcony for the flashing sword dance to begin. Night comes and I am still on the balcony. Under the moonlight, my palm tree waves and sprays needles of black, silver, and white; hundreds of shimmering lines circle and play and stay in perfect parallel.

Because the tree about which I made the error was not a sycamore, a birch, a copper beech, a stellata Leonard magnolia but a palm tree, because in other words it was a tree whose most common ground is a hemisphere not my own (southern rather than northern) or a coast not my own (west rather than east), the error may seem to be about the distance between north and south, east and west, about mistakes arising from cultural difference. Sometimes the attribution of a mistake to "cultural difference" is intended to show why caring about beauty is bad, as though if I had attended to sycamores and chestnuts

less I might have sooner seen the palminess of the
palm, this green pliancy designed to capture and re-
structure light. Nothing I know about perception
tells me how my love of the sycamore caused, or
contributed to, my failure to love the palm, since
there does not appear to be, inside the brain, a finite
amount of space given to beautiful things that can be
prematurely filled, and since attention to any one
thing normally seems to heighten, rather than diminish, the acuity with which one sees the next. Still, it
is the case that if I were surrounded every day by
hundreds of palms, one of them would have sooner
called upon me to correct my error.

Beauty always takes place in the particular, and if
there are no particulars, the chances of seeing it go
down. In this sense cultural difference, by diminish-
ing the number of times you are on the same ground
with a particular vegetation or animal or artwork,
gives rise to problems in perception, but problems in
perception that also arrive by many other paths.
Proust, for example, says we make a mistake when
we talk disparagingly or discouragingly about "life"
because by using this general term, "life," we have
already excluded before the fact all beauty and happiness, which take place only in the particular: "we
believed we were taking happiness and beauty into
account, whereas in fact we left them out and replaced them by syntheses in which there is not a

single atom of either." Proust gives a second instance of a synthetic error:

> So it is that a well-read man will at once begin to yawn with boredom when one speaks to him of a new "good book," because he imagines a sort of composite of all the good books that he has read, whereas a good book is something special, something unforeseeable, and is made up not of the sum of all previous masterpieces but of something which the most thorough assimilation ... would not enable him to discover.

Here the error arises not from cultural difference—the man is steeped in books (and steeped in life)—but from making a composite of particulars, and so erasing the particulars as successfully as if he lived in a hemisphere or on a coast that grew no books or life.

When I used to say the sentence (softly and to myself) "I hate palms" or "Palms are not beautiful; possibly they are not even trees," it was a composite palm that I had somehow succeeded in making without even ever having seen, close up, many particular instances. Conversely, when I now say, "Palms are beautiful," or "I love palms," it is really individual palms that I have in mind. Once when I was under a high palm looking up at its canopy sixty feet above

me, its leaves barely moving, just opening and clos-
ing slightly as though breathing, I gradually realized
it was looking back down at me. Stationed in the
fronds, woven into them, was a large owl whose whole
front surface, face and torso, was already angled toward the ground. To stare down at me, all she had
to do was slowly open her eyes. There was no sudden
readjustment of her body, no alarmed turning of her
head—her sleeping posture, assumed when she arrived each dawn in her palm canopy, already positioned her to stare down at anyone below, simply by
rolling open her eyes in a gesture as pacific as the
breezy breathings of the canopy in which she was
nesting. I normally think of birds nesting in cuplike
shapes where the cup is upwards, open to the sky,
but this owl (and I later found other owls entering
other palms at dawn) had discovered that the canopy
was itself a magnified nest, only it happened to be
inverted so that it cupped downward. By interleaving
her own plumage with the palm's, latching herself
into the leaves, she could hold herself out over the
sixty-foot column of air as though she were still
flying. It was as though she had stopped to sleep in
midair, letting the giant arcing palm leaves take over
the work of her wings, so that she could soar there
in the shaded sunshine until night came and she was
ready to fly on her own again.

Homer sings of the beauty of particular things. Odysseus, washed up on shore, covered with brine, having nearly drowned, comes upon a human community and one person in particular, Nausicaa, whose beauty simply astonishes him. He has never anywhere seen a face so lovely; he has never anywhere seen *any* thing so lovely. "No, wait," he says, oddly interrupting himself. Something has suddenly entered his mind. Here are the lines:

But if you're one of the mortals living here
   on earth,
three times blest are your father, your queenly
   mother,
three times over your brothers too. How often
   their hearts
must warm with joy to see you striding into
   the dances—
such a bloom of beauty. [....]
I have never laid eyes on anyone like you,
neither man nor woman . . .
I look at you and a sense of wonder takes me.
         Wait,
once I saw the like—in Delos, beside Apollo's
   altar—
the young slip of a palm-tree springing into
   the light.

There I'd sailed, you see, with a great army in
    my wake,
out on the long campaign that doomed my life
    to hardship.
That vision! Just as I stood there gazing, rapt,
    for hours . . .
no shaft like that had ever risen up from
    the earth—
so now I marvel at *you*, my lady: rapt,
    enthralled,
too struck with awe to grasp you by the knees
though pain has ground me down.[5]

Odysseus's speech makes visible the structure of perception at the moment one stands in the presence of beauty. The beautiful thing seems—is—incomparable, unprecedented; and that sense of being without precedent conveys a sense of the "newness" or "newbornness" of the entire world. Nausicaa's childlike form, playing ball on the beach with her playmates, reinforces this sense. But now something odd and delicately funny happens. Usually when the "unprecedented" suddenly comes before one, and when one has made a proclamation about the state of affairs—"There is no one like you, nothing like this, anywhere"—the mind, despite the confidently announced mimesis of carrying out a search, does not actually enter into any such search, for it is too exclusively filled with the beautiful object that stands in its presence. It is the very way the beautiful thing fills the mind and breaks all frames that gives the "never before in the history of the world" feeling.

Odysseus startles us by actually searching for and finding a precedent; then startles us again by managing through that precedent to magnify, rather than diminish, his statement of regard for Nausicaa, letting the "young slip of a palm-tree springing into the light" clarify and verify her beauty. The passage continually restarts and refreshes itself. Three key features of beauty return in the new, but chronologically prior, object of beauty.

First, beauty is sacred. Odysseus had begun (in lines earlier than those cited above) with the intuition that in standing before Nausicaa he might be standing in the presence of Artemis, and now he re-arrives at that intuition, since the young palm grows beside the altar of Delos, the birthplace of Apollo and Artemis. His speech says this: If you are immortal, I recognize you. You are Artemis. If instead you are mortal, I am puzzled and cannot recognize you, since I can find no precedent. No, wait. I do recognize you. I remember watching a tree coming up out of the ground of Delos.

Second, beauty is unprecedented. Odysseus believes Nausicaa has no precedent; then he recalls the

palm and recalls as well that the palm had no precedent: "No shaft like that had ever risen up from the
earth." The discovery of a precedent only a moment
ago reported not to exist contradicts the initial report, but at the same time it confirms the report's
accuracy since the feature of unprecedentedness stays
stable across the two objects. Nausicaa and the palm
each make the world new. Green, pliant, springing
up out of the ground before his eyes, the palm is in
motion yet stands firm. So, too, Nausicaa: she plays
catch, runs into the surf, dances an imagined dance
before her parents and brothers, yet stands firm.
When the naked Odysseus suddenly comes lurching
out onto the sand, "all those lovely girls . . . scattered
in panic down the jutting beaches. / Only Alcinous'
daughter held fast . . . and she firmly stood her
ground and faced Odysseus."

These first and second attributes of beauty are
very close to one another, for to say that something
is "sacred" is also to say either "it has no precedent"
or "it has as its only precedent that which is itself
unprecedented." But there is also a third feature:
beauty is lifesaving. Homer is not alone in seeing
beauty as lifesaving. Augustine described it as "a
plank amid the waves of the sea."[6] Proust makes a
version of this claim over and over again. Beauty
quickens. It adrenalizes. It makes the heart beat
faster. It makes life more vivid, animated, living,

worth living. But what exactly is the claim or—more to the point—exactly how literal is the claim that it saves lives or directly confers the gift of life? Neither Nausicaa nor the palm rescues Odysseus from the sea, but both are objects he sees immediately after having escaped death. Odysseus stands before Nausicaa still clotted with matter from the roiling ocean that battered him throughout Book 5, just as Odysseus stood before the young palm having just emerged out of the man-killing sea: "There I'd sailed, you see, with a great army in my wake, / out on the long campaign that doomed my life to hardship." Here again Homer re-creates the structure of a perception that occurs whenever one sees something beautiful; it is as though one has suddenly been washed up onto a merciful beach: all unease, aggression, indifference suddenly drop back behind one, like a surf that has for a moment lost its capacity to harm.

Not Homer alone but Plato, Aquinas, Plotinus, Pseudo-Dionysius, Dante, and many others repeatedly describe beauty as a "greeting." At the moment one comes into the presence of something beautiful, it greets you. It lifts away from the neutral background as though coming forward to welcome you—as though the object were designed to "fit" your perception. In its etymology, "welcome" means that one comes with the well-wishes or consent of the person or thing already standing on that ground. It is as though the welcoming thing has entered into, and consented to, your being in its midst. Your arrival seems contractual, not just something you want, but something the world you are now joining wants. Homer's narrative enacts the "greeting."[7] Odysseus hears Nausicaa even before he sees her. Her voice is green: mingling with the voices of the other children, it sounds like water moving through lush meadow grass. This greenness of sound becomes the fully articulated subject matter of her speech when she later directs him through her father's groves, meadows, blossoming orchards, so he can reach their safe inland hall, where the only traces of the ocean are the lapis blue of the glazed frieze on the wall and the "sea-blue wool" that Nausicaa's mother continually works. Nausicaa's beauty, her welcoming countenance, allows Odysseus to hope that he will be made welcome in "the welcome city," "welcome Scheria"—that "generous King Alcinous" and the Phaeacian assembly will receive him, as in fact they do, with "some mercy and some love."

Odysseus has made a hymn to beauty. One may protest that this description tonally overcredits Odysseus since—something that has so far not been mentioned—Odysseus is here being relentlessly strategic. He has a concrete, highly instrumental goal. He must get Nausicaa to lead him to safety. The lines immediately preceding his hymn of praise show him "slyly" calculating how to approach her. How should he walk? Stand? Speak? Should he hold himself upright or kneel on the ground before her? Should he grasp her by the knees or keep his distance, stand reverently back? But just as his hymn to beauty can be seen as an element subordinate to the larger frame of his calculation for reentering the human community, so the narrative of calculation can be seen as subordinate to the hymn of beauty. The moment of coming upon something or someone beautiful might sound—if lifted away from Odysseus's own voice and arriving from a voice outside him—like this: "You are about to be in the presence of something life-giving, lifesaving, something that deserves from you a posture of reverence or petition. It is not clear whether you should throw yourself on your knees before it or keep your distance from it, but you had better figure out the right answer because this is not an occasion for carelessness or for leaving your own postures wholly to chance. It is not that beauty is life-threatening (though this attribute has sometimes been assigned it), but instead that it is life-affirming, life-giving; and therefore if, through your careless approach, you become cut off from it, you will feel its removal as a retraction of life. You will fall back into the sea, which even now, as you stand there gazing, is only a few feet behind you." The framework of strategy and deliberation literalizes, rather than undermines, the claim that beauty is lifesaving.

Sacred, lifesaving, having as precedent only those things which are themselves unprecedented, beauty has a fourth feature: it incites deliberation. I have spoken of Odysseus's error toward Nausicaa. But one could just as easily see Odysseus's error as committed against the palm: seeing Nausicaa, he temporarily forgets the palm by the altar, injuring it by his thoughtless disregard and requiring him at once to go on to correct himself. The hymn to Nausicaa's beauty can instead be called a palinode to the beauty of the palm. By either account, Odysseus starts by making an error.

So far error has been talked about as a cognitive event that just happens to have beauty—like anything else—as one of its objects. But that description, which makes error independent of beauty, may itself be wrong. The experience of "being in error" so inevitably accompanies the perception of beauty that it begins to seem one of its abiding structural features. On the one hand, something beautiful—a blossom, a friend, a poem, a sky—makes a clear and self-evident appearance before one: this feature can be called "clear discernibility" for reasons that will soon be elaborated. The beauty of the thing at once fills the perceiver with a sense of conviction about that beauty, a wordless certainty—the this! here! of Rilke's poetry. On the other hand, the act of perceiving that seemingly self-evident beauty has a built-in liability to self-correction and self-adjustment, so much so that it appears to be a key element in whatever beauty is. This may explain why, as noticed earlier, when the informal experiment is conducted of asking people about intellectual errors, they do not readily remember ever having made one (or, more accurately, they are sure they have made one but do not happen to remember what it is); whereas when you ask them about errors in beauty, they seem not only to remember one but to recall the process of correction in vivid sensory detail. Something beautiful immediately catches attention yet prompts one to judgments that one then continues to scrutinize, and that one not infrequently discovers to be in error.

Something beautiful fills the mind yet invites the search for something beyond itself, something larger or something of the same scale with which it needs to be brought into relation. Beauty, according to its critics, causes us to gape and suspend all thought. This complaint is manifestly true: Odysseus does stand marveling before the palm; Odysseus is similarly incapacitated in front of Nausicaa; and Odysseus will soon, in Book 7, stand "gazing," in much the same way, at the season-immune orchards of

King Alcinous, the pears, apples, and figs that bud on one branch while ripening on another, so that never during the cycling year do they cease to be in flower and in fruit. But simultaneously what is beautiful prompts the mind to move chronologically back in the search for precedents and parallels, to move forward into new acts of creation, to move conceptually over, to bring things into relation, and does all this with a kind of urgency as though one's life depended on it. So distinct do the two mental acts appear that one might believe them prompted by two different species of beauty (as Schiller argued for the existence of both a "melting" beauty and an "energetic" beauty)[8] if it weren't for the fact that they turn up folded inside the same lyric event, though often opening out at chronologically distinct moments.

One can see why beauty—by Homer, by Plato, by Aquinas, by Dante (and the list would go on, name upon name, century by century, page upon page, through poets writing today such as Gjertrud Schnackenberg, Allen Grossman, and Seamus Heaney)—has been perceived to be bound up with the immortal, for it prompts a search for a precedent, which in turn prompts a search for a still earlier precedent, and the mind keeps tripping backward until it at last reaches something that has no precedent, which may very well be the immortal. And one can see why beauty—by those same artists, philosophers, theologians of the Old World and the New—has been perceived to be bound up with truth. What is beautiful is in league with what is true because truth abides in the immortal sphere. But if this were the only basis for the association, then many of us living now who feel skeptical about the existence of an immortal realm might be required to conclude that beauty and truth have nothing to do with one another. Luckily, a second basis for the association stands clearly before us: the beautiful person or thing incites in us the longing for truth because it provides by its compelling "clear discernibility" an introduction (perhaps even our first introduction) to the state of certainty yet does not itself satiate our desire for certainty since beauty, sooner or later, brings us into contact with our own capacity for making errors. The beautiful, almost without any effort of our own, acquaints us with the mental event of conviction, and so pleasurable a mental state is this that ever afterwards one is willing to labor, struggle, wrestle with the world to locate enduring sources of conviction—to locate what is true. Both in the account that assumes the existence of the immortal realm and in the account that assumes the nonexistence of the immortal realm, beauty is a starting place for education.

Hymn and palinode—conviction and consciousness of error—reside inside most daily acts of encountering something beautiful. One walks down a street and suddenly sees a redbud tree—its tiny heart-shaped leaves climbing out all along its branches like children who haven't yet learned the spatial rules for which parts of the playground they can run on. (Don't they know they should stay on the tips of the twigs?) It is as though one has just been beached, lifted out of one ontological state into another that is fragile and must be held onto lest one lose hold of the branch and fall back into the ocean. Like Odysseus, one feels inadequate to it, lurches awkwardly around it, saying odd things to the small leaves, wishing to sing to them a hymn or, finding oneself unable, wishing in apology to make a palinode. Perhaps like Dante watching Beatrice, one could make a sonnet and then a prose poem explaining the sonnet; or, like Leonardo looking at a violet, one could make a sketch, then another, then another; or like Lady Autumn, listening with amazement to a stanza Keats has just sung her, one could sit there patiently staring moment after moment, hour by hour. Homer was right: beauty is lifesaving (or life-creating as in Dante's title *La vita nuova*, or life-altering as in Rilke's imperative "You must change your life"). And Homer was right: beauty incites deliberation, the search for precedents. But what about the immortal, about which Homer may or may not have been right? If we look at modern examples of the palinode for a missing precedent, does the plenitude and aspiration for truth stay stable, even if the meta-physical referent is in doubt?

Matisse never hoped to save lives. But he repeatedly said that he wanted to make paintings so serenely beautiful that when one came upon them, suddenly all problems would subside. His paintings of Nice have for me this effect. My house, though austere inside, is full of windows banking onto a garden. The garden throws changing colors into the chaste rooms—lavenders, pinks, blues, and pools of green. One winter when I was bereft because my garden was underground, I put Matisse prints all over the walls—thirteen in a single room. All winter long I applied the paintings to my staring eyes, and now they are, in retrospect, one of the things that make my former disregard of palm trees so startling. The precedent behind each Nice painting is the frond of a palm; or, to be more precise, each Nice painting is a perfect cross between an anemone flower and a palm frond. The presence of the anemone I had always seen—in the mauve and red colors, the abrupt patches of black, in the petal-like tissue of curtains, slips, parasols, and tablecloths, in the small pools of color with sudden drop-offs at their edges. But I

completely missed what resided behind these surfaces, what Odysseus would have seen, the young slip
of a palm springing into the light.

The signature of a palm is its striped light. Palm
leaves stripe the light. The dyadic alternations of leaf
and air make the frond shimmer and move, even
when it stays still, and if there is an actual breeze,
then the stripings whip around without ever losing
their perfect alignment across the full sequence. Matisse transcribes this effect to many of the rooms in
the Nice paintings. Here is the structure of one en-
titled *Interior, Nice, Seated Woman with a Book*, where the
arcings and archings of the fronds are carried in the
rounding curves of the curtain and chair and woman.
The striped leaf-light is everywhere in the room, in
the louvered slats of the slanted window, in the louvered slats of the straight window, in the louvered
slats reflecting in the glass window, in the striped

blue-and-white cloth on the lower right and its mirrored echo, in the woman's striped robe, lifting out from its center like an array of fronds from a stalk, and in the large bands of color in the architectural features of the room. On the upper left, lifting high above the woman, a single curved frond cups outward, its red, blue, and green leaf colors setting the palette for the rest of the room: it registers the botanical precedent, in case the small surface of the actual black-green palm (visible in the upper half of the window and indicated in my sketch by dark ink) is missed. Light trips rapidly across the surface of the room: in out in, out in out in, out off on off, on out off in, on off on off. It feathers across the eye, excites

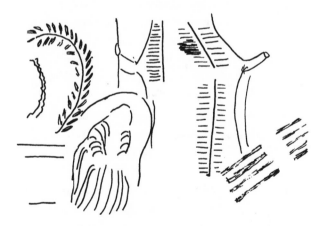

Interior, Nice. Seated Woman with a Book

it, incites in it saccadic leaps and midair twirls ("retinal arabesques," my friend calls them). It is as though the painting were painted with the frond of a palm, or as though the frond were just laid down on the canvas, as though it swished across the canvas, leaving prints of itself here there here there here there.

In *My Room at the Beau Rivage*, the striping, the stationary equivalent of shimmering, is accomplished through the pink-and-yellow wallpaper stripes and the curved lines of the satin chair, where the leaf-light is so concentrated it simply whites out in one section. The pliant chair, like the woman in *Seated Woman with a Book*, is the newborn palm tree, the place where light pools and then spills outward in all directions. Like silver threads appearing and disappearing behind the cross threads of a weaving— not a finished weaving but one whose making is just now under way—the silver jumps of our eyes trip in unison across the stripes, appearing and disappearing beneath the latticing of the guide threads. It is as though white sea-lanes have been drawn on the surface of the ocean and across them Nereids dive in and out.

Missing the print of the palm seems remarkable. The thing so capaciously and luminously dispersed throughout the foreground of the room is concretely specified at the very back of (almost as if behind) the

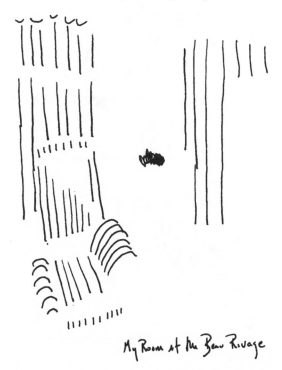

My Room at the Beau Rivage

painting. The palm is present in all, or almost all, of the Nice paintings. But the amount of surface that is dedicated to the actual tree, as opposed to the palmy offspring stripings inside the room, is tiny—one-thirtieth of the canvas in *Seated Woman with a Book*, one-fiftieth of the canvas in *My Room at the Beau Rivage*, and similar small fractions in others of the 1920s, such as *The Morning Tea, Woman on a Sofa, Still Life: 'Les*

Pensées de Pascal,' Vase of Flowers in Front of the Window, in each of which the tree occupies between one-fiftieth and one sixty-third of the full surface.

Further, the tree's individuated fronds are themselves seldom visible, and the leaves, never. A curtain may be striped; a wall may be striped; a bowl of flowers may be striped; a floor may be striped; a human figure may be striped; a table, bed, or chair may be striped. The fronds are the one thing to

WOMAN ON A SOFA

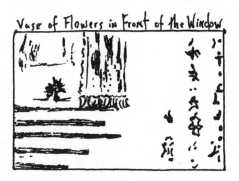

Vase of Flowers in Front of the Window

which stripes are disallowed, except perhaps in *"Les Pensées de Pascal"* where (on close inspection of the very small tree) the green branchings have a cupped pink underside that sets in motion, inside the room, the soft blocks of gray and pink where the curtain overlaps the windowsill, and the hot pink and gray stripes on the sill below. More typically the tree canopy looks like a knob of broccoli, sometimes lacks a trunk, and may even be positioned in the lower half

of the painting. It provides just a fleeting acknowl-
edgment of the fact that it is the precedent that sets
in motion all the light-filled surfaces in the foreground. The tree is the only thing in the paintings to
which the palm-style is not applied, just as when
Matisse includes a bowl of actual anemones or nas-
turtiums or fritillarias in his paintings, it is often the
one thing to which the anemone-style, nasturtium-
style, or fritillaria-style (everywhere else filling the
room) will be disallowed.

But at least one painting from the Nice period—
The Painter and His Model, Studio Interior (1919)—explicitly announces the fact that the palm frond is the
model from which, or more accurately the instrument with which, Matisse paints. Perhaps the palm
is here openly saluted and seized because the painting is overtly about the act of painting. The room is
full of sunlight. Yellow. Cream. Gold. White. These
colors cover two-thirds of its surface, which is also
awash with lavenders and reds falling in sun-filled
stripes from the curtains, the walls, the man, the
table, the chair, the dresser. The palm in the window
is still only a small fraction of the surface, one thirty-
fifth, but unlike many other Nice paintings, it is here
stark, self-announcing. The palm now has emphatic
fronds. It is brown, like the painter's brush, which
has only a shaft and no brush, and so seems supplied
by the tree, as though the palm were a continuation

The Painter and His Model
1919

of the tool he holds, interrupted by the woman's body (the woman who is technically the model referred to in the title, though the palm seems more model than she). The palm seems not just the model, the thing that inspires him or the thing he aspires to copy, but much more material in its presence. It is what he reaches out for, closes his hand around, and presses down on the surface of the canvas he is lashing with light. It is a graphic literalization of "brush," "to brush," a brush with beauty. Because the palmy stripings incite the silver cross-jumps of light over our face and eyes, it is as though the painting in turn paints us, plaiting braids of light across the surface of our skin.

Other Nice paintings depicting the act of composition similarly register the palm as instrument. The woman painter in *The Morning Session* (1924) wears a yellow-and-black striped dress that covers her torso, lap, and legs—the vertical stripes become horizontal when they reach her lap, raying out like sunlight before becoming vertical again as they turn at her knees and drop to the floor. She sits in front of a red-and-white striped wall, and long vertical bands of peach

streak down the window, down the walls, and down the back of her painting. Because of the angle at which she sits, the brush with which she paints (like the man's in *The Painter and His Model*) has only a shaft and no brush, but by good luck there stand directly above her hand the open fronds, the luxurious canopy brush, of a distant palm. This vision of creation extends to auditory composition. The musician's bow in *Young Woman Playing the Violin in Front of the Open Window* (1923) is also completed and continued by the fronds of the palm outside her window, turning her bow into a brush. She is safely held in the lap of the striped walls on three sides. Above her head,

Young Woman Playing the Violin in Front of the Open Window

the huge open window—open sky, open sea, open sail, open palm—seems the picture of the airy music she is playing, a picture painted with the brush of her bow.

Three decades later, Matisse still paints palms in windows, but now as the fulsome, fully saluted precedent. The pictures seem Odyssean palinodes to the once insufficiently acknowledged tree. By 1947 the

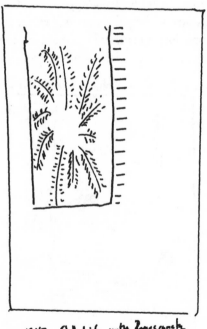

1947 *Still Life with Pomegranate*

palm fills not one sixty-third or one-fiftieth or one-thirtieth of the painting but one-quarter. By 1948 it fills one-half. In both pictures it has become the central subject. Formerly deprived of the very style it inspired, it is now the single thing in the picture to which the leaf-light striping is emphatically applied. The palm in *Still Life with Pomegranate* is composed of hundreds of green stripes against light blue. The

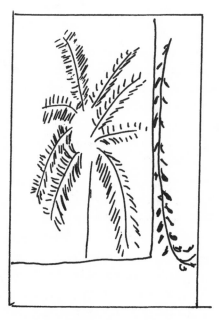

1948 Interior with Egyptian Curtain

palm in *Interior with Egyptian Curtain* is composed of hundreds upon hundreds of stripes in black, green, yellow, white. On the wall inside the 1948 canvas *Large Interior in Red* hangs a black-and-white picture with a palm outside the window and another palm inside the room—palm fronds painted with a palm frond on a palm frond—the painter's material, instrument, and subject.

I began here with the way beautiful things have a forward momentum, the way they incite the desire to bring new things into the world: infants, epics, sonnets, drawings, dances, laws, philosophic dialogues, theological tracts. But we soon found ourselves also turning backward, for the beautiful faces and songs that lift us forward onto new ground keep calling out to us as well, inciting us to rediscover and recover them in whatever new thing gets made. The very pliancy or elasticity of beauty—hurtling us forward and back, requiring us to break new ground, but obliging us also to bridge back not only to the ground we just left but to still earlier, even ancient, ground—is a model for the pliancy and lability of consciousness in education. Matisse believed he was painting the inner life of the mind; and it is this elasticity that we everywhere see in the leaf-light of his pictures, the pliancy and palmy reach of the capacious mind. Even when the claim on behalf of immortality is gone, many of the same qualities—plenitude, inclusion—are the outcome.

It sometimes seems that a special problem arises for beauty once the realm of the sacred is no longer believed in or aspired to. If a beautiful young girl (like Nausicaa), or a small bird, or a glass vase, or a poem, or a tree has the metaphysical in behind it, that realm verifies the weight and attention we confer on the girl, bird, vase, poem, tree. But if the metaphysical realm has vanished, one may feel bereft not only because of the giant deficit left by that vacant realm but because the girl, the bird, the vase, the book now seem unable in their solitude to justify or account for the weight of their own beauty. If each calls out for attention that has no destination beyond itself, each seems self-centered, too fragile to support the gravity of our immense regard.

But beautiful things, as Matisse shows, always carry greetings from other worlds within them. In surrendering to his leaf-light, one is carried to other shorelines as inevitably as Odysseus is carried back to Delos. What happens when there is no immortal realm behind the beautiful person or thing is just what happens when there *is* an immortal realm

behind the beautiful person or thing: the perceiver is
led to a more capacious regard for the world. The
requirement for plenitude is built-in. The palm will
always be found (whether one accidentally walks out
onto a balcony, or follows at daybreak the flight path
of an owl, or finds oneself washed up in front of
Nausicaa or a redbud or *Seated Woman with a Book*)
because the palm is itself the method of finding. The
material world constrains us, often with great benefi-
cence, to see each person and thing in its time and
place, its historical context. But mental life doesn't
so constrain us. It is porous, open to the air and light,
swings forward while swaying back, scatters its
stripes in all directions, and delights to find itself
beached beside something invented only that morning or instead standing beside an altar from three
millennia ago.

   This very plasticity, this elasticity, also makes
beauty associate with error, for it brings one face-to-
face with one's own errors: momentarily stunned by
beauty, the mind before long begins to create or to
recall and, in doing so, soon discovers the limits of
its own starting place, if there are limits to be found,
or may instead—as is more often the case—uncover
the limitlessness of the beautiful thing it beholds.
Though I have mainly concentrated here on failures
of plenitude and underattribution—mistakes that

involve not seeing the beauty of something—the same outcomes can be arrived at by the path of over-attribution, as registered in the poems about error by Dickinson, Hopkins, Shakespeare. This genre of error, however, has the peculiarity that when the beautiful person or thing ceases to appear beautiful, it often incites the perceiver to repudiate, scorn, or even denounce the object as an invalid candidate or carrier of beauty. It is as though the person or thing had not merely been beautiful but had actually made a claim that it was beautiful, and further, a claim that it would be beautiful forever.[9] But of course it is we—not the beautiful persons or things themselves (Maud Gonne, Mona Lisa, "Ode to a Nightingale," Chartres, a columbine, a dove, a bank of sweet pea, a palm tree)—who make announcements and prom-ises to one another about the enduring beauty of these beautiful things. If a beautiful palm tree one day ceases to be so, has it defaulted on a promise? Hopkins defends the tree:

> No, the tropic tree
> Has not a charter that its sap shall last
> Into all seasons, though no Winter cast
> The happy leafing.

The temptation to scorn the innocent object for ceasing to be beautiful might be called the temptation against plenitude; it puts at risk not the repudiated object but the capaciousness of the cognitive act.

Many human desires are coterminous with their object. A person desires a good meal and—as though by magic—the person's desire for a good meal seems to end at just about the time the good meal ends. But our desire for beauty is likely to outlast its object because, as Kant once observed, unlike all other pleasures, the pleasure we take in beauty is inexhaustible. No matter how long beautiful things endure, they cannot out-endure our longing for them. If the beauty of an object lasts exactly as long as the life of the object—the way the blue chalice of a morning glory blossom spins open at dawn and collapses at noon—it will not be faulted for the disappearance of its beauty. Efforts may even be made to prolong our access to its beauty beyond its death, as when Aristotle, rather than turning away from a dying iris blossom, tracks the changing location of its deep colors, and Rilke, rather than turning away from the rose at the moment it breaks apart, describes the luxurious postures the flower adopts in casting down its petals.

But if the person or thing outlives its own beauty—as when a face believed ravishing for two years no longer seems so in the third, or a favorite vase one day ceases to delight, or a poem beloved in the decade when it is written becomes incomprehensible to those who read it later—then it is sometimes not just turned away from but turned upon, as though it has enacted a betrayal. But the work that beautiful persons and things accomplish is collectively accomplished, and different persons and things contribute to this work for different lengths of time, one enduring for three millennia and one enduring for only three seconds. A vase may catch your attention, you turn your head to look at it, you look at it still more carefully, and suddenly its beauty is gone. Was the beauty of the object false, or was the beauty real but brief? The three-second call to beauty can have produced the small flex of the mind, the constant moistening, that other objects—large, arcing, flexuous—will more enduringly require. We make a mistake, says Seamus Heaney, if, driving down a road between wind and water, overwhelmed by what we see, we assume we will see "it" better if we stop the car. It is there in the passage. When one goes on to find "better," or "higher," or "truer," or "more enduring," or "more widely agreed upon" forms of beauty, what happens to our regard for the less good, less high, less true, less enduring, less universal instances? Simone Weil says, "He who has gone farther, to the very beauty of the world itself, does not love them any less but much more deeply than before."

I have tried to set forth the view here that beauty really is allied with truth. This is not to say that what is beautiful is also true. There certainly are objects in which "the beautiful" and "the true" do converge, such as the statement "$1 = 1$." This may be why, though the vocabulary of beauty has been banished or driven underground in the humanities for the last two decades, it has been openly in play in those fields that aspire to have "truth" as their object—math, physics, astrophysics, chemistry, biochemistry— where every day in laboratories and seminar rooms participants speak of problems that are "nice," theories that are "pretty," solutions that are "beautiful," approaches that are "elegant," "simple." The participants differ, though, on whether a theory's being "pretty" is predictive of, or instead independent of, its being "true."[10]

But the claim throughout these pages that beauty and truth are allied is not a claim that the two are identical. It is not that a poem or a painting or a palm tree or a person is "true," but rather that it ignites the desire for truth by giving us, with an electric brightness shared by almost no other uninvited, freely arriving perceptual event, the experience of conviction and the experience, as well, of error. This liability to error, contestation, and plurality—for which "beauty" over the centuries has so often been belittled—has sometimes been cited as evidence of its falsehood and distance from "truth," when it is instead the case that our very aspiration for truth is its legacy. It creates, without itself fulfilling, the aspiration for enduring certitude. It comes to us, with no work of our own; then leaves us prepared to undergo a giant labor.

PART TWO

On Beauty and
Being Fair

THE BANISHING of beauty from the humanities in the last two decades has been carried out by a set of political complaints against it. But, as I will try to suggest, these political complaints against beauty are themselves incoherent. Beauty is, at the very least, innocent of the charges against it, and it may even be the case that far from damaging our capacity to attend to problems of injustice, it instead intensifies the pressure we feel to repair existing injuries. I will try to set forth a sketch of the way aesthetic attributes exert this pressure on us.

When I say that beauty has been banished, I do not mean that beautiful things have themselves been banished, for the humanities are made up of beautiful poems, stories, paintings, sketches, sculpture, film, essays, debates, and it is this that every day draws us to them. I mean something much more modest: that conversation about the beauty of these things has been banished, so that we coinhabit the space of these objects (even putting them inside us, learning them by heart, carrying one wedged at all times between the upper arm and the breast, placing as many as possible into our bookbags) yet speak about their beauty only in whispers.

The Political Arguments against Beauty
Are Incoherent

The political critique of beauty is composed of two distinct arguments. The first urges that beauty, by preoccupying our attention, distracts attention from wrong social arrangements. It makes us inattentive, and therefore eventually indifferent, to the project of bringing about arrangements that are just. The second argument holds that when we stare at something beautiful, make it an object of sustained regard, our act is destructive to the object. This argument is most often prompted when the gaze is directed toward a human face or form, but the case presumably applies equally when the beautiful thing is a mourning dove, or a trellis spilling over with sweet pea, or a book whose pages are being folded back for the first time. The complaint has given rise to a generalized discrediting of the act of "looking," which is charged with "reifying" the very object that appears to be the subject of admiration.

Whatever merit either of these arguments has in and of itself, it is clear at the outset that they are unlikely both to be true since they fundamentally contradict one another. The first assumes that if our "gaze" could just be coaxed over in one direction and made to latch onto a specific object (an injustice in need of remedy or repair), that object would benefit from our generous attention. The second assumes that generous attention is inconceivable, and that any object receiving sustained attention will somehow suffer from the act of human regard. Because the two complaints so fundamentally contradict one another, evidence that can be brought forward on behalf of the first tends to call into question the accuracy of the second; and conversely, evidence that can be summoned up on behalf of the second works to undermine the first.

If, for example, an opponent of beauty eventually persuades us that a human face or form or a bird or a trellis of sweet pea normally suffers from being looked at, then when the second opponent of beauty complains that beauty has caused us to turn away from social injustice, we will have to feel relieved that whatever harm the principals are now suffering is at least not being compounded by our scrutiny of them.[1] If instead we are persuaded that beauty has distracted us from suffering, and that our attention to that suffering will help reduce the harm, we will have to assume that human perception, far from poisoning each object it turns toward, is instead fully capable of being benign.

It seems that the two opponents of beauty have a greater quarrel with each other than with us and should perhaps be encouraged to press forward their claims, since they will together eliminate both grounds of opposition and leave us free once more to speak of beauty. But seasons come and go, decades are passing, and the two arguments—by never being brought together in a single space—continue to flourish. So, as bad-tempered as the effort may seem, some time must be given here to contesting the two views.

The opponents of beauty could conceivably defend the consistency of their two views. They might say the following. It is not that one of us holds perception to be benign and the other holds perception to be malicious: we are speaking of two distinguishable kinds of perception. It is pleasure-filled perception (as when one listens to the mourning dove terracing its sweet calls or the crowing of the cock on a distant hillside) that is morally bad; and it is aversive perception (as when one turns on the radio and hears, with distress, one point of view being systematically suppressed) that is morally good. But it seems almost inconceivable that anyone with affection for human beings could wish on them so harsh an edict, permitting only perceptions that bring discomfort. More important, there is no way to be in a high state of alert toward injustices—to subjects that, because they entail injuries, will bring distress—without simultaneously demanding of oneself precisely the level of perceptual acuity that will forever be opening one to the arrival of beautiful sights and sounds. How will one even notice, let alone become concerned about, the inclusion in a political assembly of only one economic point of view unless one has also attended, with full acuity, to a debate that is itself a beautiful object, full of arguments, counterarguments, wit, spirit, ripostes, ironies, testing, contesting; and how in turn will one hear the nuances of even this debate unless one also makes oneself available to the songs of birds or poets?

One other possible way our two opponents might claim they can reconcile their apparently contradictory complaints about beauty would be to say that passive perception—looking or hearing without any wish to change what one has seen or heard (as often happens in the presence of the beautiful)—is unacceptable; whereas instrumental perception—looking or hearing that is prelude to intervening in, changing, what one has seen or heard (as happens in the presence of injustice)—is good. But a moment's reflection will show that this is just a slight rephrasing of the earlier proposal that pleasurable perception is morally bad and aversive perception is morally good. Further, it seeks to make the whole sensorium utilitarian, an outcome laudable only in high emergencies.

It is the argument of this chapter that beauty, far from contributing to social injustice in either of the two ways it stands accused, or even remaining neutral to injustice as an innocent bystander, actually assists us in the work of addressing injustice, not only by requiring of us constant perceptual acuity—high dives of seeing, hearing, touching—but by the more direct forms of instruction sketched in the next part of the chapter. The sketch counters both grounds of attack, but because it more directly addresses the first (the enduring claim that beauty makes us inattentive to justice), it may be helpful to address here very briefly the second (the relatively recent complaint that beauty enlists the perceiver into an act of perception that reifies). It has two major weaknesses.

First, the complaint is often formulated in such a way that, in its force and scope, it seems to be generalized to all objects of beauty—the poems of John Donne or John Keats, mother-of-pearl poppies, gods from both the East and the West, human faces, buildings—even though the particular instances explicitly cited are almost always confined to one particular site of beauty, the beauty of persons. Even if we could be persuaded that looking at beautiful human faces and forms were harmful to the persons we seem to be admiring, it is not clear why the entire world of natural and artifactual, physical and metaphysical beauty should be turned away from. It seems that at most we should be obligated to give up the pleasure of looking at one another.

No detailed argument or description is ever brought forward to justify this generalization, yet the generalization has worked to silence conversations about beauty. If this critique or the other critiques against beauty were crisply formulated as edicts or treatises with sustained arguments and examples, the incoherence would be more starkly visible and the influence correspondingly diminished. They exist instead as semiarticulate but deeply held convictions that—like snow in a winter sky that keeps materializing in the air yet never falls or accumulates on the ground—make their daily way into otherwise lively essays, articles, exams, conversations. Suddenly, out of the blue, someone begins to speak about the way a poet is reifying the hillside or painting or flower she seems to be so carefully regarding.

One way of seeing the weakness of the generalization is to test it across different categories of beautiful objects, categories of objects whose beauty is beloved not just by people in Western countries but by people everywhere. The beauty of persons is honored throughout the world, but so, too, is the beauty of gods, the beauty of gardens, the beauty of poems.

So let us take these four—gods, gardens, persons, and poems—and hold one of them, persons, out for the moment, looking only at the other three.

The argument that "noticing beauty brings harm to the thing noticed" makes no sense if the object is not itself susceptible to harm, as seems to be true of something that is all-powerful such as a god or non-sentient such as a poem. Many stories are told about attempts made to put the gods at risk, but the stories are usually about the immunity of the deity, the foolhardiness of the infidel. Those attacking the god do not, in any event, do so by paying attention to the god's beauty. Pentheus expresses sneering contempt for the effeminate beauty of the double-gendered Dionysus; it is instead Dionysus's rhapsodic worshipers who chant encomiums to the beauty of his hair, his body, his voice, his dance, his wine, his theatrical rituals. The face and body of Jesus occasion Aquinas's famous setting forth of the threefold division of beauty into integrity, proportion, and *claritas*—key terms for subsequent aesthetic debate over many centuries up through the conversations of Joyce's Stephen Dedalus and his friend Lynch. Jehovah prohibits anyone from looking at him face-to-face, but only the human perceiver, not Jehovah, is endangered by the act of looking; and though God is not seen, the Hebrew Scriptures revere the beauty of his countenance and his righteousness: "And let the beauty of the Lord our God be upon us."[2] So it is again with Hindu and Buddhist deities. The lotus shapes of the lips, eyes, hands, postures are sculpted into stone and wood by the adoring hands of worshipers, not the hands of detractors.

Noticing beauty, then, does no harm in cases where the object is either perfect (gods) or nonsentient (poem, vase). Further, as the examples suggest, it may even confer a benefit by perpetuating the religion in acts of worship or perpetuating the poem by making certain it does not disappear or get revised by those incapable of seeing its beauty. A vase crafted by Gallé—in whose surface dusky blue plums and purple leaves hang in the soft brown light—can, although nonsentient, be harmed by being mishandled. Noticing its beauty increases the possibility that it will be carefully handled.

Now it may be objected that a less beautiful poem or vase or god may, by receiving less attention, receive less careful protection. This objection inevitably comes up at exactly this moment in conversations about beauty: we saw it earlier in the complaint that what accounted for my disregard of a culturally distant tree was my absorption with sycamores and chestnuts. The complaint can, as a shorthand, be called the problem of lateral disregard, the problem that whatever benefits accrue to an object through its being the focus of our attention are not being equally enjoyed by nearby objects in the same class. The phenomenon of lateral disregard will be returned to in more detail later; but for now it is important to see the following. First, whatever the truth of this complaint, it does nothing to confirm the particular complaint that is before us at the present moment— namely, the complaint that our gaze brings harm to gods, poems, gardens, persons, and vases. The problem of lateral disregard assumes our gaze is good, and worries about our failure to distribute it out to objects that are similar to the one we are staring at, but which lack the perfect features that obligate us to stare. Like the political complaint about inattention to problems of social injustice to which it is related, it explicitly confirms the value of human attention. Second, it may well be the case that a less perfectly crafted poem or political debate is less likely to be preserved for posterity; but it is not at all self-evident that this lack of protection is the necessary counterpart of our focus upon the more highly crafted poem or political debate, or that it was in any way prompted by them. If I was about to place a vase on a wide safe ledge and then, finding one more beautiful, I consigned the first vase to a careless spot, we might have a case. But it seems more likely that the concern demanded by the perfect vase or god or poem introduced me to a standard of care that I then began to extend to more ordinary objects (perhaps I began to notice and worry, for the first time, about my neglect of the ordinary object and, inspecting it more closely, may now even discover that it is not ordinary). Far from subtracting or robbing fragility from the ordinary vase, the extraordinary vase *involuntarily* introduced me to the recognition that vases are fragile, and I then *voluntarily* extended the consequences of that recognition to other objects in the same category. I may see that reverence is due not only to a beautiful god but to the god's mother or to nearby angels; that it is not just the poet's best poem that should be published but even the penultimate, nearly-as-beautiful draft, that the flawed political debate should be perpetuated for posterity as part of the large public record of great and lapsed moments of assembly. The benefit of the extraordinary is twofold: first, in the demands it (without our invitation) places on us on its own behalf; second, in the pressure it exerts toward extending the same standard laterally. This pressure toward the distributional is an unusual feature of beautiful persons or things. The fact that it may be one beholder who is singing a hymn of praise to the first object, while it is a second beholder who, as though in harmony, is now demanding that love now be equally accorded to a lateral object, should not discourage us from seeing the two as a composite event sponsored by the beautiful object itself.

But for now we need to return to the frame of our
concern, whether the charge that staring harms the
person being stared at can fairly be generalized to
other categories of beautiful things. We have so far
spoken about beautiful things to which the argument
about perceptual damage seems inapplicable because
they are beyond harm (either because perfect and
omnipotent or because nonsentient like an artwork).
But of course some things are neither omnipotent
nor nonsentient but highly vulnerable and simultaneously highly sentient—or more accurately, since
there are no degrees of sentience, unnegotiably alive.
Persons are the most pressing example, and it may
be for this very reason that the argument about the
hazards of gazing originates right here, at the site of
persons.

Is, then, the aliveness of something a ground on
which we might wish to banish it as a candidate for
beauty? One can, even in the sites looked at a moment ago, see why this avenue might be in error; for
it cannot have escaped our attention that even when
the objects we were speaking about were omnipotent
or nonsentient, their being perceived as beautiful
seemed to bring them to life or to make them life-
like. In some cases, maybe in all, this can be called a
mimesis of life: for each morning when the sun rises
and reaches the windowsill where the Gallé vase sits,
the amber glass swells with light; the blue-and-

brown plums drift in and out of the purple leaves, their veins and stems now flecked with life. The almost-aliveness of a beautiful object makes its abrasive handling seem unthinkable. The mind recoils— as from a wound cut into living flesh—from the possibility that the surface of Jan Brueghel the Elder's painting *Flower Stems in a Clay Vase* should be cut, torn, or roughly touched. Its surface has been accorded the gift of life: this can have nothing to do with the subject, the live flowers, for—look at them, jonquils, roses, fritillaria, tulips, irises, peonies, hyacinths, lily—they were already cut even as the painter painted them into their place inside the vase; and the same mental recoil would be felt if the surface that were roughly touched depicted only a pair of discarded shoes or one of Turner's groundless mists or Klee's colors. The surface of the canvas has become, in the standard of protection we accord it, semisentient. Stone statues of gods, too, in the moment of being revered, come to life, as in Rilke's poems where the mouth of Apollo trembles and the eyebrows of Buddha lift.

We saw in Part One that the moment of perceiving something beautiful confers on the perceiver the gift of life; and now we begin to see that the moment of perceiving beauty also confers on the object the gift of life. The pacific quality of beauty comes in part from the reciprocal, life-granting pact. But we were about to look at sites of beauty—persons and gardens—that do not just, under special circumstances, acquire the gift of lifelikeness but are themselves unequivocally alive; and the question is, are these actually alive things inappropriate subjects for our admiring gaze?

We must still leave to the side the highly puzzling site of persons, because the present question is this: even if it is the case that we can be persuaded to stop looking at persons, ought the negative account of harmful looking be extended to other sites such as gods, poems, and—the site now before us— gardens? Because flowers are alive, they are (unlike omnipotent or nonsentient things) susceptible to damage; but a moment's reflection shows the impossibility of concluding that this damage is brought about by our perception of them, and the deep oddity of banishing them from our regard. Gardens exist for the sake of being beautiful and for the sake of having that beauty looked at, walked through, lingered in. In this one respect the sentient site of gardens and the nonsentient (or only sentient-like) site of poems are alike; for poems too—as well as other art objects such as glass vases and paintings—are brought into being in order to place their beauty in the field of human regard. Prohibiting attention to the beauty of gardens or poems therefore seems even more peculiar than prohibiting attention to the beauty of gods and persons.[3] Gods of many traditions are held to be beautiful, but gods do not come into existence to be beautiful: their beauty simply follows from, or is part of, their perfection and cannot be decoupled or held independent from it. If we ceased praising their beauty,[4] the love of them might become less fervent and widespread; but it does not seem our silence would be fatal. Persons, too, though often beautiful, cannot be said to exist for the sake of being beautiful, even if we must grant that at the moment the parents conceive a child, each wishes the beauty of the beloved, already in the world, to enter the world a second time. Of course it is imaginable that someone perceiving a beautiful garden might then trample on it,[5] just as someone perceiving beautiful persons or paintings might then attempt to destroy them; but so many laws and rules are already being broken by these acts that it is hard to comprehend why, rather than bringing these rules and laws to bear on the problem, the rules of perceiving need to be altered to accommodate the violator. Excluding the beauty of gardens and poems from perception would more swiftly destroy them than any occasional act of trampling. Only if the sestinas and the perennials could outlive the edict could there even continue to be gardens or poems.

By now we should be willing to agree that the general form of the complaint—"the perceiver reifies the object of perception"—makes little sense. It does not apply to gods, poems, and gardens. Nor has any evidence been brought forward to suggest its applicability to other sites. The habit of broadening this complaint from the site of persons to the world at large appears to be baseless. Let us agree that we will give it up. Attention to the beauty of all things (gods, gardens, poems—and also the moon, the Milky Way, individual stars, the daylit sky, birds, birdsongs, musical instruments, meadows, dances, woven cloth, stones, staircases, good prose certainly, airplanes of course, mathematical proofs, the sea, its surf, its spray) will be permitted, and only attention to the site of persons will be prohibited. But what about this site of persons?

I suggested at the outset that the complaint had two weaknesses. The first weakness was its generalization from the site of persons to all other things. The second weakness is the claim it makes about the site of persons itself.

People spend so much time noticing one another that the practice will no doubt continue regardless of the conclusions we arrive at about beauty. But many arguments can be made to credit the pleasure people take in one another's countenance. Staring, as we earlier saw, is a version of the wish to create; it is directly connected to acts of drawing, describing, composing, lovemaking. It is odd that contemporary accounts of "staring" or "gazing" place exclusive emphasis on the risks suffered by the person being looked at, for the vulnerability of the perceiver seems equal to, or greater than, the vulnerability of the person being perceived. In accounts of beauty from earlier centuries, it is precisely the perceiver who is imperiled, overpowered, by crossing paths with someone beautiful. Plato gives the most detailed account of this destabilization in the *Phaedrus*. A man beholds a beautiful boy: suddenly he is spinning around in all directions. Publicly unacceptable things happen to his body. First he shudders and shivers. Then sweat pours from him. He is up, down, up, down, adopting postures of worship, even beginning to make sacrifices to the boy, restrained only by his embarrassment at carrying out so foolish an activity in front of us. Now he feels an unaccountable pain. Feathers are beginning to emerge out of his back, appearing all along the edges of his shoulder blades. Because this plumage begins to lift him off the ground a few inches, he catches glimpses of the immortal realm. Nonetheless, it cannot be denied that the discomfort he feels on the inside is matched by how ridiculous he looks on the outside. The beholder in Dante's *Vita nuova* is equally at risk. Coming face-to-face with Beatrice, Dante undergoes a violent trembling. All his senses go into a huddle, alarmed at the peril to which he has just exposed them. Soon he is so immobilized he might be mistaken for "a heavy inanimate object."

It is hard—no matter how dedicated one is to the principle of "historical difference"—to account for the discrepancy between the aura of radical vulnerability beholders were assigned in the past and the aura of complete immunity they are assigned today. Someone committed to historicism might shrug and say, "We just no longer see beauty in the same way." But how can that be an acceptable answer if—as an outcome of this newly acquired, wretched immunity—people are asking us to give up beauty altogether? A better answer might be to say not that we see the beauty of persons differently but that we do not see it at all. Perhaps only if one spins momentarily out of control, or grows feathers, or begins to write a sonnet can one be said to have seen the beauty of another person. The essentialist who believes beauty remains constant over the centuries and the historicist or social constructionist who believes that even the deepest structures of the soul are susceptible to cultural shaping have no need, when confronting the present puzzle, to quarrel with one another. For either our responses to beauty endure unaltered over centuries, or our responses to beauty are alterable, culturally shaped. And if they are subject to our willful alteration, then we are at liberty to make of beauty what we wish. And surely what we should wish is a world where the vulnerability of the beholder is equal to or greater than the vulnerability of the person beheld, a world where the pleasure-filled tumult of staring is a prelude to acts that will add to the beauty already in the world—acts like making a poem, or a philosophic dialogue, or a divine comedy; or acts like repairing an injury or a social injustice. Either beauty already requires that we do these things (the essentialist view) or we are at liberty to make of beauty the best that can be made—a beauty that will require that we do these things.

I suggested above that in those cases where a perceiver "gazes" with immunity at a person (and convincing instances have been documented by literary critics and art historians), two descriptions are possible: one claims, "In our era we see the beauty of persons in a way different from the way Plato and Dante did"; the other claims, "In our era we no longer see the beauty of persons." If the second is true, then what should be blamed for those occasions on which the person looked at is put at risk is not "seeing beauty" but "failing to see beauty"; and what should be urged is not the banishing of beauty but beauty's immediate return. A third description would say that the documented occasions, though real enough, are aberrations, and that "in our era we still see the beauty of persons the way Plato and

Dante did." There is much to support this view: not just the number of new inventions and the number of people who, like Rilke (scratched, then killed, by the thorn of a rose), have died for beauty; but also the evidence of everyday experience. For it simply is the case—isn't it?—that each of us has, upon suddenly seeing someone beautiful, tripped on the sidewalk, broken out in a sweat of new plumage, dropped packages (as though offering a gift or sacrifice)—all while the bus we were waiting for pulls up and pulls away.

If today's beholder were suddenly offered the chance, while keeping his own features, to have a beauty as great as that of the person looked at, would the beholder decline that invitation? If we really believe that "beholders are all-powerful" and "persons beheld are powerless," then wouldn't we decline the offer? Why place oneself at risk by becoming beautiful, and why convert the already beautiful person into a coldly immune surveillant? But might one not instead happily accept? Proust watches the glowing red-haired woman serving milk at the train stop and wishes to accompany her in her daily labor in order to keep her in his field of vision; but he has the equally ardent wish to be included in *her* field of vision, "to feel that I was known to her, had my place in her thoughts." This, too, is why our "appalling" Odysseus washes: he scrubs the cakes of "brackish scurf" from his head and body, rubs himself with oil, and permits Athena's hand to wash over him like the hand of a smith who "washes gold over beaten silver." Athena's washing magnifies his size and stature, and "down from his brow / she ran his curls like thick hyacinth clusters / full of blooms." At last, Odysseus is ready to reenter Nausicaa's field of vision:

> And down to the beach he walked and
> sat apart,
> glistening in his glory, breathtaking, yes,
> and the princess gazed in wonder . . .

It may be that one reason beautiful persons and things incite the desire to create is so that one can place something of reciprocally great beauty in the shared field of attention. No hyacinth clusters can give homely Socrates the beauty of Phaedrus, but the speeches Socrates composes for Phaedrus have the same outcome. When Dante composes poems in response to Beatrice's beauty, it is as though he has bathed on the Phaeacian shore.

But we are pursuing a misleading track here, for these are pairs of lovers; and it is important to contemplate the way beauty works not only with respect to someone one loves, but also with respect to the large array of beautiful persons walking through the public sphere. As we will eventually see, the fact that we look at beautiful persons and things without wishing to be ourselves beautiful is one of the key ways in which—according to philosophers like Simone Weil and Iris Murdoch—beauty prepares us for justice. It is then more useful simply to ask the nature of the relation between the person who pursues beauty and the beauty that is pursued. But as this question involves not just persons but many other sites of beauty, it must be postponed a short time.

Before leaving the site of persons, we must recall that we were here looking at only one complaint, the complaint that we might, by looking at such persons, bring them harm. But there are, of course, other arguments less political but equally antagonistic to the site of persons, such as the notion that beautiful persons do not deserve to be attended to for their beauty. Sometimes this idea of undeservingness is urged on the grounds that their beauty is natural: such persons were born with it, lazily inheriting it through no labor or merit of their own. (This argument is not very strong since so many things we unembarrassedly admire—great math skill, a capacity for musical composition, the physical agility of a dancer or speed of an athlete—entail luck at birth.) With equal energy the idea of undeservingness is urged on the grounds that such beauty is artifactual:

such persons spend hours running along the beach, plaiting their hair into tiny braids, adorning themselves with beads, bracelets, oil, arrays of color. (This argument is also not very strong since we normally admire feats of artifactual labor, the formation of good government, a well-run newspaper, a twelve-year labor of self-education.) The two complaints contradict one another—one proposing that it is not the natural but the artifactual that should be honored, and the other proposing that it is not the artifactual but the natural that should be honored. More important, they together contradict the complaint we were considering: they say beautiful persons do not deserve to be looked at, whereas the complaint we were wrestling with says beautiful persons deserve not to be looked at (for their own safety). Although, therefore, we have limited ourselves to political arguments, we find—when we step off the straight and narrow path of our present inquiry—an incoherence equal to the one that lies straight ahead.

That straight path—to recover our bearings—has had two parts. First, we saw that the argument that perceiving beauty brings harm is, at most, applicable to the site of persons and cannot be generalized to gods, gardens, poems. Second, we saw that the argument does not stand up even with respect to persons since, if anything, the perceiver is as vulnerable as, or more vulnerable than, the person looked at. The objection is, therefore, neither site-specific nor legitimately diffused out to other sites.

Two other revelations have come forward, almost on their own, that will help us, as we begin to turn now from the negative arguments on behalf of beauty (showing the incoherence of the political complaints against it) to the positive arguments (showing how beautiful things assist us in remedying injustice). We saw that the fact that something is perceived as beautiful is bound up with an urge to protect it, or act on its behalf, in a way that appears to be tied up with the perception of its lifelikeness. This observation first emerged in connection with objects that themselves have no bodily sentience, such as a painted canvas, but that seem to acquire it, or a mimetic form of it, at the very moment of our regarding them as beautiful. Left unanswered was the question of exactly how this lifelikeness bears on persons, flowers, and birds, which can have unevenness of beauty but cannot have an unevenness of aliveness.

The second attribute that emerged was the pressure beauty exerts toward the distributional. This pressure manifests itself in what has been called the problem of lateral disregard, the worry that inevitably follows in the wake of observing the beautiful:

"something's receiving attention" seems to involve "something else's not receiving attention." The structure of perceiving beauty appears to have a two-part scaffolding: first, one's attention is involuntarily given to the beautiful person or thing; then, this quality of heightened attention is voluntarily extended out to other persons or things. It is as though beautiful things have been placed here and there throughout the world to serve as small wake-up calls to perception, spurring lapsed alertness back to its most acute level. Through its beauty, the world continually recommits us to a rigorous standard of perceptual care: if we do not search it out, it comes and finds us. The problem of lateral disregard is not, then, evidence of a weakness but of a strength: the moment we are enlisted into the first event, we have already become eligible to carry out the second. It may seem that in crediting the enduring phenomenon of beauty with this pressure toward distribution, we are relying on a modern notion of "distribution." But only the word is new. Plato's requirement that we move from "eros," in which we are seized by the beauty of one person, to "caritas," in which our care is extended to all people, has parallels in many early aesthetic treatises, as when Boethius is counseled by Lady Philosophy, and later, Dante is counseled by Virgil to listen only to a song whose sensory surface will let one move beyond its own compelling features to a more capacious sphere of objects. The metaphysical plane behind the face or song provided the moral urgency for insisting upon this movement away from the particular to the distributional (or as it was called then, in a word that is often now berated, the universal). The vocabulary, but not the ethical direction, differs from the distributional mandate.

One final matter will enable us to move forward to the positive claims that can be spoken on behalf of beauty. We saw that the two political arguments are starkly incompatible with one another; and we also saw along the way that if we move into the intricacy of any one argument and one site—such as the site of persons—the objections on this more minute level are also wildly contradictory. If we were to move not into the intricate interior but outside to the overarching framework—if we were, in other words, to move outside the political arguments and contemplate their relation to the nonpolitical arguments used to assault beauty—we would come face-to-face with the same incoherence.

A case in point is the demotion of beauty that has come about as a result of its juxtaposition with the sublime. It is not the sublime that is incoherent, nor even the way in which the sublime systematically demotes beauty that is incoherent. What is incoherent is the relation between the kinds of claims that are made by this demotion and the political arguments looked at earlier.

The sublime has been a fertile aesthetic category in the last twenty years and has been written about with such intricacy that I will sketch its claims only in the briefest form, so that those unfamiliar with it will know what the aesthetic is. At the end of the eighteenth century, writers such as Kant and Burke subdivided the aesthetic realm (which had previously been inclusively called beauty) into two realms, the sublime and the beautiful. Kant's early work, the *Observations on the Feeling of the Beautiful and Sublime*, gives so straightforward a list that it can be recited, nearly verbatim, as a shorthand, even though it does not convey the many complications of Kant's own later writing on the subject, nor of the important writings following it. In the newly subdivided aesthetic realm, the sublime is male and the beautiful is female. The sublime is English, Spanish, and German; the beautiful is French and Italian. The sublime resides in mountains, Milton's Hell, and tall oaks in a sacred grove; the beautiful resides in flowers and Elysian meadows. The sublime is night, the beautiful day. "The sublime *moves*" (one becomes "earnest . . . rigid . . . astonished"). "Beauty *charms*." The sublime is dusk, "disdain for the world . . . eternity"; the beautiful is lively gaiety and cheer. The sublime is great; the beautiful "can also be small." The sublime is simple; the beautiful is multiple. The sublime is principled, noble, righteous; the beautiful is compassionate and good-hearted.[6]

Why should this bifurcation have dealt such a blow to beauty (a blow not intended by the original writers of the treatises nor by later writers on the sublime)? The sublime occasioned the demotion of the beautiful because it ensured that the meadow flowers, rather than being perceived in their *continuity* with the august silence of ancient groves (as they had when the two coinhabited the inclusive realm of beauty),[7] were now seen instead as a *counterpoint* to that grove. Formerly capable of charming or astonishing, now beauty was the not-astonishing; as it was also the not-male, the not-mountainous, the not-righteous, the not-night. Each attribute or illustration of the beautiful became one member of an oppositional pair, and because it was almost always the diminutive member, it was also the dismissible member.

Furthermore, the path to something beyond both meadow flower and mighty tree, something detachable from their concrete surfaces—one might call it, as Kant did, eternity; or one might instead describe it as the mental realm where, with or without a god's help, the principles of justice and goodness hold sway—suddenly ceased to be a path of free movement and became instead a path lined with obstructions. In its earlier continuity with the meadow flower, the magnificent tree had itself assisted, or at least not interrupted, the passage from blossom to the sphere of just principles; now the magnificent tree served as a giant boulder, a locked gate, a border guard, jealously barring access to the realm that had been reconceived as adjacent to itself and thus as only its own to own. The sublime now prohibited, or at least interrupted, the easy converse between the diminutive and the distributive.

One can see how oddly, yet effectively, the demotion from the sublime and the political demotion work together, even while deeply inconsistent with one another. The sublime (an aesthetic of power) rejects beauty on the grounds that it is diminutive, dismissible, not powerful enough. The political rejects beauty on the grounds that it is too powerful, a power expressed both in its ability to visit harm on objects looked at and also in its capacity to so overwhelm our attention that we cannot free our eyes from it long enough to look at injustice. Berated for its power, beauty is simultaneously belittled for its powerlessness.

The multiple, opposing assaults on beauty have worked in a second way. The sublime—by which I mean the outcomes that followed from dividing a formerly unitary realm into the sublime and the beautiful—cut beauty off from the metaphysical, permitting it to inhabit only the ground of the real. Then the political critique—along with a closely related moral critique and a critique from realism— come forward to assert that beauty (forever discomforting mortals with its idealized conceptions) has no place on the ground of the real. Permitted to inhabit neither the realm of the ideal nor the realm of the real, to be neither aspiration nor companion, beauty comes to us like a fugitive bird unable to fly, unable to land.

Beauty Assists Us in Our Attention to Justice

The positive case that can be made on behalf of beauty has already begun to emerge into view and will stand forth more clearly if we place before ourselves the question of the relation between the beholder and the object beheld. The question can best be posed if we, for a moment, imagine that we are speaking not about the person who comes upon beauty accidentally, or the person who—after valiantly resisting beauty for all the reasons one should be warned against it—at last succumbs, but instead about a person who actively seeks it out.

What is it that such a person seeks? What precisely does one hope to bring about in oneself when one opens oneself to, or even actively pursues, beauty?

When the same question is asked about other enduring objects of aspiration—goodness, truth, justice—the answer seems straightforward. If one pursues goodness, one hopes in doing so to make oneself good. If one pursues justice, one surely hopes to be able one day to count oneself among the just. If one pursues truth, one wishes to make oneself knowledgeable. There is, in other words, a continuity between the thing pursued and the pursuer's own attributes. Although in each case there has been an enhancement of the self, the undertaking and the outcome are in a very deep sense unself-interested since in each case the benefits to others are folded into the nature of my being good, bearing knowledge, or acting fairly. In this sense it may have been misleading to phrase the question in terms of a person's hopes for herself. It would be more accurate to say that one cannot further the aims of justice without (whether one means to or not) placing oneself in the company of the just. What this phrasing and the earlier phrasing have in common, the key matter, is the continuity between the external object and the person who is dedicated to it.

But this continuity does not seem to hold in the case of beauty. It does not appear to be the case that one who pursues beauty becomes beautiful. It may even be accurate to suppose that most people who pursue beauty have no interest in becoming themselves beautiful. It would be hard to make the same description of someone pursuing the other objects of aspiration: could one pursue truth if one had no interest in becoming knowledgeable? This would seem like quite a feat. How exactly would one go about that? Would there be a way to approach goodness while keeping oneself free of becoming good? Again, a path for doing so does not immediately suggest itself. And the same difficulties await us if we try to come up with a way of furthering the goals of justice while remaining ourselves outside its reach.

Now there are at least three ways in which one might wish to say that the same kind of continuity between beauty and its beholder exists. The beholder, in response to seeing beauty, often seeks to bring new beauty into the world and may be successful in this endeavor. But those dedicated to goodness or truth or justice were also seeking to carry out acts that further the position of these things in the world; the particular alteration of self they underwent (the thing for which we are seeking a parallel) is something additional to the fact that they supplemented the world. A second answer is to say that beholders of beautiful things themselves become beautiful in their interior lives: if the contents of consciousness are full of the calls of birds, mental pictures of the way dancers move, fragments of jazz pieces for piano and flute, remembered glimpses of ravishing faces, a sentence of incredible tact and delicacy spoken by a friend, then we have been made intensely beautiful. Still, this cannot be a wholly satisfying reply since though the beautiful object may, like the beholder, have internal beauty, it also has external features; this externality has long been held to be crucial to what beauty is, and even to its particular way of turning us toward justice. But there is a third answer that seems more convincing.

One key source of continuity between beholder and beheld became strikingly evident when we earlier saw the way each affirms the aliveness of the other. First we saw in the opening part that beauty is for the beholder lifesaving or life-restoring—a visionary fragment of sturdy ground: the palm tree on the sand of Delos, the floating plank that Augustine holds onto, the branch Noah sees flying through the sky. Then, when we moved from the first to the second part, it became clear that this act of conferring life had a reciprocal counterpart. The thing perceived, the beautiful object, has conferred on it by the beholder a surfeit of aliveness: even if it is inanimate, it comes to be accorded a fragility and consequent level of protection normally reserved for the animate; if inanimate, like a poem, it may, by being memorized or read aloud to others, thereby be lent the aliveness of the person's own consciousness. If

what is beheld is instead a person, he or she may
sponsor—literally—the coming into the world of a
newborn, so that the person now stands companioned by additional life; the more general manifestation of this same phenomenon is visible in the way
one's daily unmindfulness of the aliveness of others
is temporarily interrupted in the presence of a beautiful person, alerting us to the requirements placed
on us by the aliveness of all persons, and the same
may take place in the presence of a beautiful bird,
mammal, fish, plant. What has been raised is not the
level of aliveness, which is already absolute, but one's
own access to the already existing level of aliveness,
bringing about, if not a perfect match, at least a less
inadequate match between the actual aliveness of
others and the level with which we daily credit them.
Beauty seems to place requirements on us for attending to the aliveness or (in the case of objects)
quasi-aliveness of our world, and for entering into its
protection.

Beauty is, then, a compact, or contract between
the beautiful being (a person or thing) and the perceiver. As the beautiful being confers on the perceiver the gift of life, so the perceiver confers on the
beautiful being the gift of life. Each "welcomes" the
other: each—to return to the word's original meaning—"comes in accordance with [the] other's will."[8]
Why this reciprocal pact should assist us in turning

toward problems of justice will be looked at in conjunction with the second positive attribute of beauty, the pressure toward distribution that we came upon in attending to the problem of lateral disregard, the way in which the requirements involuntarily placed on us by something extraordinary have as a counterpart the shift toward the voluntary extension of these same perceptions. The compatibility between this distributive feature and a turn toward justice will not be hard to discover, since the language of "distribution" (unlike the language of "aliveness") is already an abiding part of the way we every day think and speak about justice.

The notion of a pact here again comes into play. A single word, "fairness," is used both in referring to loveliness of countenance and in referring to the ethical requirement for "being fair," "playing fair" and "fair distribution." One might suppose that "fairness" as an ethical principle had come not from the adjective for comely beauty but instead from the wholly distinct noun for the yearly agricultural fair, the "periodical gathering of buyers and sellers." But it instead—as scholars of etymology have shown—travels from a cluster of roots in European languages (Old English, Old Norse, Gothic), as well as cognates in both Eastern European and Sanskrit, that all originally express the aesthetic use of "fair" to mean "beautiful" or "fit"—fit both in the sense of "pleasing to the eye" and in the sense of "firmly placed," as when something matches or exists in accord with another thing's shape or size. "Fair" is connected to the verbs "vegen" (Dutch) and "fegen" (German) meaning "to adorn," "to decorate," and "to sweep." (One recalls Tolstoy, during his decade of deepest commitment to social justice, beginning each day by sweeping his room; as one may think, as well, of the small brooms in Japanese gardens, whose use is sacred, reserved to the priests.) But "fegen" is in turn connected to the verb "fay," the transitive and intransitive verb meaning "to join," "to fit," "to unite," "to pact."[9] "Pact" in turn—the making of a covenant or treaty or agreement—is from the same root as "pax, pacis," the word for peace.

Although the two attributes of beauty can each be described in isolation from the other, they together constitute a two-part cognitive event that affirms the equality of aliveness. This begins within the confined circumference of beholder and beheld who exchange a reciprocal salute to the continuation of one another's existence; this two-member salute becomes, by the pressures against lateral disregard, dispersed out so that what is achieved is an inclusive affirmation of the ongoingness of existence, and of one's own responsibility for the continuity of existence. Our status as the bearer of rights, our equality of aliveness, does not rely on the existence of beautiful meadows or skies or persons or poems to bring it about; nor, once there are laws and codified rights in place, should beautiful meadows and skies be needed to keep it in view, but—as will be unfolded below— matters that are with difficulty kept legible in one sphere can be assisted by their counterpart in the other.

How this takes place will be clarified if we look first at the connection between beauty as "fairness" and justice as "fairness," using the widely accepted definition by John Rawls of fairness as a "symmetry of everyone's relations to each other." The discussion will then turn to the idea of "aliveness," a word that, though it enters our discussions of justice less openly and less often than words such as "fairness" and "equality," is what is centrally at stake in, and served by, both spheres.

Fairness as "A Symmetry of Everyone's Relation to One Another"

One day I ran into a friend, and when he asked me what I was doing, I said I was trying to explain how beauty leads us to justice. (It happens that this friend is a philosopher and an economist who has spent many years inquiring into the relation between famine and forms of procedural justice such as freedom of the press. He also tracked demographic figures in

Asia and North Africa that revealed more than one hundred million missing women and showed a long-standing practice of neglecting the health of girls.) Without pausing, he responded that he remembered being a child in India and coming upon Aristotle's statement that justice was a perfect cube:[10] he had been completely baffled by the statement, except he knew it had something to do with equality in all directions.

Happening to find myself sometime later walking beside another friend, and again pressed to describe what I was up to, I said I was showing that beauty assists us in getting to justice, and—perhaps because the subject seemed out of keeping with the morning's seaside glee—I for some reason added, "But *you* surely don't believe this." (He is a political philosopher who inquires into the nature of deliberative processes, and has established a series of alternative models for ethics; he served in British intelligence during the Second World War and in the Foreign Office during the period of the Marshall Plan.) "No," he agreed, still laughing, and high above the cresting waves, for we were walking on a steep dune, he cited with delight a proclamation about beauty's inevitable descent into bohemia. "Except, of course," he added, turning suddenly serious, and holding out his two large hands, "analogically, by what they share: balance and the weighing of both sides."

The speed and immediacy with which Amartya Sen and Stuart Hampshire spoke is indicative of the almost self-evident character of the argument that will be made here: that beautiful things give rise to the notion of distribution, to a lifesaving reciprocity, to fairness not just in the sense of loveliness of aspect but in the sense of "a symmetry of everyone's relation to one another."

When we speak about beauty, attention sometimes falls on the beautiful object, at other times on the perceiver's cognitive act of beholding the beautiful thing, and at still other times on the creative act that is prompted by one's being in the presence of what is beautiful. The invitation to ethical fairness can be found at each of these three sites, and so each will be looked at in turn: the first in statements made by classical philosophers, Plato and Augustine; the second, in observations by mid-twentieth-century philosophers Simone Weil and Iris Murdoch; and the third in an account given by turn-of-the-millennium philosopher Andreas Eshete, whose work is divided between the practical task of establishing constitutional rights in Ethiopia and theoretical writings about fraternity: he argues that of the revolutionary triad—liberty, equality, fraternity—it is fraternity (often omitted from our descriptions) that underwrites liberty and equality, and hence also fraternity that underwrites liberal theories of justice.

As this list suggests, I have in this one section of the discussion placed the burden of illustration on those who—by their writings, their practice, or both— have dedicated themselves first and foremost to questions of justice, rather than on those who have dedicated themselves first and foremost to beauty; for the reader may feel that anyone who sets out in the morning to defend beauty will surely by nightfall have arrived at the strategy of claiming that beauty assists justice, whereas political philosophers are un- likely to put justice at risk by placing it in beauty's hands unless they deem it prudent to do so.

When we begin at the first of the three sites—the site of the beautiful object itself—it is clear that the attribute most steadily singled out over the centuries has been "symmetry." Some eras single it out almost to the exclusion of all else (remarkably, one such period is the decade of the 1990s),[11] whereas others insist that it is not symmetry alone but symmetry companioned by departures and exceptions from itself that makes a piece of music, a face, or a land- scape beautiful (as in the nineteenth-century ro- mantic modification of the principles of eighteenth- century neoclassicism). The feature, despite these variations in emphasis, never ceases to be, even in eras that strive to depart from it, the single most enduringly recognized attribute. But what happens when we move from the sphere of aesthetics to the sphere of justice? Here symmetry remains key, particularly in accounts of distributive justice and fairness "as a symmetry of everyone's relation to one another." It was this shared feature of beauty and justice that Amartya Sen saluted in the figure of the cube, equidistant in all directions, and that Stuart Hampshire again saluted in the figure of scales, equally weighted in both directions.

But why should we not just accept Hampshire's formulation that this is an "analogy," a feature they share, rather than the much stronger formulation, that it is the very symmetry of beauty which leads us to, or somehow assists us in discovering, the symmetry that eventually comes into place in the realm of justice? One answer is this: in periods when a human community is too young to have yet had time to create justice, as well as in periods when justice has been taken away, beautiful things (which do not rely on us to create them but come on their own and have never been absent from a human community) hold steadily visible the manifest good of equality and balance.

Which of the many early writers—such as Parmenides, Plato, Boethius, each of whom saw the sphere, because equidistant in all directions, as the most perfect of shapes—shall we call on for illustration? Here is Augustine thinking about musical rhythm in the sixth book of *De Musica*. He is not

setting forth an attribute of distributive justice; he is
not recommending that medieval hierarchies be
overthrown and replaced by democracies; yet present to his mind—as present to the mind of the
writers of scores of other ancient treatises on cubes,
spheres—is a conviction that equality is the heart of
beauty, that equality is pleasure-bearing, and that
(most important in the shift we are seeking to undertake from beauty to justice) equality is the morally
highest and best feature of the world. In other words,
equality is set forth as the thing of all things to be
aspired to:

> The higher things are those in which equal-
> ity resides, supreme, unshaken, unchangeable,
> eternal.

> This rhythm [that, like certain principles of
> arithmetic, can be elicited from a person who
> has never before been tutored in it] is immuta-
> ble and eternal, with no inequality possible in
> it. Therefore it must come from God.

> Beautiful things please by proportion, *numero*,
> . . . equality is not found only in sounds for the
> ear and in bodily movements, but also in visible
> forms, in which hitherto equality has been
> identified with beauty even more customarily
> than in sounds.

It is easy to love colours, musical sounds, *voces*, cakes, roses and the body's soft, smooth surface, *corpora leniter mollia*. In all of them the soul is in quest of nothing except equality and similitude.

Water is a unity, all the more beautiful and transparent on account of a yet greater similitude of its parts ... on guard over its order and its security. Air has still greater unity and internal regularity than water. Finally the sky ... has the greatest well-being.[12]

Can we, could Augustine, did any reader, ever emerge from this cascade of paragraphs—of which only a small filigree is given here—without having their yearning for, their commitment to, equality intensified? No claim is being made here about the length of time—a year, a century, a millennium—it might take for the same equality to inhere in social relations. All that is claimed is that the aspiration to political, social, and economic equality has already entered the world in the beauty-loving treatises of the classical and Christian periods, as has the readiness to recognize it as beautiful if and when it should arrive in the world.

To return, then, to the question of whether the symmetry in beauty and that in justice are analogous, or whether instead the first leads to the second, the answer already proposed can be restated and expanded through Augustine's idiom. Imagine, then, a world that has blue sky, musical sounds, cakes, roses, and the body's soft, smooth surface; and now imagine further that this world also has a set of just social arrangements and laws that (like Augustine's water) by their very consistency stand guard over and secure themselves. The equality residing in the song-filled sky light and the equality residing in the legal arrangements need not be spoken about as anything other than analogous, especially since the laws (both written and applied with a consistency across all persons) are now themselves beautiful. But remembering there was a time antecedent to the institution of these laws, and recognizing also that this community will be very lucky if, in its ongoing existence through future history, there never comes an era when its legal system for a brief period deteriorates, we can perceive that ongoing work is actively carried out by the continued existence of a locus of aspiration: the evening skies, the dawn chorus of roosters and mourning doves, the wild rose that, with the sweet pea, uses even prison walls to climb on. In the absence of its counterpart, one term of an analogy actively calls out for its missing fellow; it presses on us to bring its counterpart into existence, acts as a lever in the direction of justice. An analogy is inert and at rest only if both terms are present in the world; when one term is absent, the other becomes an active conspirator for the exile's return.

But there is also a second way in which even in a community that has both fair skies and fair legal arrangements, the sky still assists us. For the symmetry, equality, and self-sameness of the sky are present to the senses, whereas the symmetry, equality, and self-sameness of the just social arrangements are not. In the young worlds and in the lapsed worlds, justice was not available to the senses for the simple reason that justice was not in the world. But even when justice comes into the world, it is not ordinarily sensorially available. Even once it has been instantiated, it is seldom available to sensory apprehension, because it is dispersed out over too large a field (an entire town or entire country), and because it consists of innumerable actions, almost none of which are occurring simultaneously. If I step out my front door, I can see the four petals of each mother-of-pearl poppy, like small signal flags: two up, two down; three up, one down; all four up; all four down. I cannot see that around the corner a traffic rule is being followed; I cannot see that over on the other side of town, the same traffic rule is being followed. It is not that the following of the traffic rule is not material: it is that its justice, which is not in a solitary location but in a consistency across all locations and in the resulting absence of injury, is not sensorially visible, as are the blades of the poppy, even though each of its component members (each car, each driver, each road surface with its white dividing line, each blinking light) is surely as material as the fragile poppy. It is the very exigencies of materiality, the susceptibility of the world to injury, that require justice, yet justice itself is outside the compass of our sensory powers.

Now it is true that once a law or constitutional principle is formulated that protects the arrangement, the sentence can be taken in in a single visual or acoustical glance; and this is one of the great powers of bestowing on a diffuse principle a doctrinal location.[13] Having a phrase at hand—"the First Amendment," "the Fourth Amendment"— gathers into itself what is, though material, outside the bounds of sensory perception. Sometimes it may even happen that a just legal principle has the good fortune to be formulated in a sentence whose sensory features reinforce the availability of the principle to perception: "We hold these truths to be self-evident, that all men are created equal. . . ." The sentence scans. The cadence of its opening sequence of monosyllables shifts suddenly forward to the polysyllabic "self-evident," the rapidity of completion adrenalizing the line, as though performing its own claim (it sounds self-verifying). The table has been cleared for the principle about to be announced. Now the sen-

tence starts over with the stark sequence of monosyllables ("that all men are") and the faster-paced, polysyllabic, self-verifying "created equal." The repeated
cadence enables each half of the sentence to author-
ize the other. Who is the "we" empowered to de-
clare certain sentences true and self-evident? the
"we" who count themselves as one another's equals.
We more often speak of beautiful laws than of beautiful social arrangements because the laws, even when
only pieces of language, have a sensory compression
that the diffusely scattered social arrangements do
not have, and it is this availability to the senses that
is also one of the key features of beauty.

But it may happen on occasion that the fair political arrangement itself (not just the laws prescribing
it or guaranteeing it) *will* be condensed into a time
and space where it becomes available to the senses,
and then—like Augustine's water, sky, cakes, and
roses—its beauty is visible. This may be true in a
great assembly hall, where the representatives delib-
erate in a bowl of space available to perception. Now
the claim has been made that the principle of rhythmic equality (which we were a moment ago enjoying in Augustine) did in the ancient Greek world
also take place in the sphere of social arrangements
and—this next step is crucial—in social arrangements contracted down into a small enough physical
space that it was available to sensory perception:

namely, the trireme ships, the ships whose 170 oars and 170 oarsmen could, like a legislative assembly, be held within the small bowl of visual space of which a human perceiver is capable, and whose rhythmic striking of the water, in time with the pipeman's flute, could also be held within the finite auditory compass of a perceiver. But we have not yet arrived at the claim, and it is this: out of the spectacle of the trireme ship, Athenian democracy was born:

> Democracy was instituted or strengthened in substantial degree by the need for a large navy of relatively poor but free citizens, who were paid for their ship duty by the state. The democratic reforms of Periclean Athens . . . shifted the domestic political and military balance of power toward the poor and the navy. . . . [At] the height of democratic government, trireme rowers were full citizens. With 170 rowers in each of at least 200 ships, no fewer than 30,000 supporters of democracy [were present], generally from the lower classes.[14]

Drawing on the Athenian constitution (which designates the oarsmen as "the men who gave the city its power"), on writings by Thucydides, Xenophon, Euripides, on the almost complete correspondence between those Greek city-states that had democracies and those Greek city-states that had navies, both historians of the ancient world[15] and democratic theorists have affirmed the association. Here again the meaning of "fair" in the sense of loveliness of countenance and "fair" in the sense of distribution converge: for the root "fegen" means not just "to sweep" but also "to strike" or "to beat," actions that appear to be connected to the sweeping or striking motion of the oars.

Euripides gives a visionary account of oarsmen striking and sweeping the silver surface of the sea, according to the pace of the aulete's piped song, the dolphins cresting and diving to the same flashing meter, as though in fraternal salute. The piper is named by Euripides as the musician of all musicians, Orpheus; and this alliance between poetic meter and rowing has endured over many centuries. Rilke reports that he came to understand "the position of the poet, his place and effect within time" only when he sailed in a ship whose powerful rowers counted aloud, and whose singer would send a "series of long floating sounds" out over the water.[16] Seamus Heaney, reading aloud from his new translation of *Beowulf*, interrupted himself at the moment when the ships enter the water, saying, it is here that the poem becomes most beautiful and alive, because of the deep connection (observed by Robert Graves) between the rhythm of poetry and the rhythm of rowing—the motion of the oars, "the dip and drag."

We can be forgiven, in a discussion of beauty, for not wishing to speak about war ships, whether the Greek triremes or the shells of the Danes and Geats; but since our subject is also justice, the issue of force must of necessity come forward. Even beauty alone would eventually have required us to speak of it. The particular topic at hand is the way that symmetry across social relations is usually invisibly dispersed out over a large expanse but in rare and exceptional moments comes to be compressed down into a small enough space to be directly available to sensory perception. We can find peaceful illustrations. Historians of the nineteenth-century United States have shown that the parade is a peculiarly American invention, designed to display within the contracted space of the city street the plurality of citizenry moving together on an equal footing.[17] Rowing races, too, take place on level waters: they have been called the "ideal egalitarian" or democratic sport, not only because of the pluralistic crowds that gathered on the riverbanks, but because of the plurality of class and gender among the rowers. Champions included customhouse workers and mechanics like the Biglin brothers, whose famous faces now stare out at us from Thomas Eakins's paintings, and whose races first attracted widespread attention when the brothers issued an open challenge to the "gentlemen-only" rowing clubs of Britain.[18] As poets have felt in their own meter the beat of the rower's heart and the pull of the rower's arms, so Eakins described the painter moving through the world on the surface of his canvas like a rower gliding over water in his weightless scull.[19]

But what makes street parades, river races, and playing fields fair is precisely a dividing up, an equal parsing out, of the unsightly means of force. Beauty is pacific: its reciprocal salute to continued existence, its pact, is indistinguishable from the word for peace. And justice stands opposed to injury: "injustice" and "injury" are the same word. The best guarantee of peace would seem to be the absence of injuring power from the world (including the absence of discrepancies in bodily size that would enable one person to bring physical force to bear on another). The second-best form (and the first-best form that has ever been available to us) is that whatever means of force exist be equally divided among us all, a distribution of force that has often been called the "palladium of civil rights," for it enables each person to stand guard over and secure the nature of the whole. What, during the first two centuries of the United States, was said to distinguish the distributed militia of democracy from the executive "standing" army of tyranny was that it was, in both the ethical and the aesthetic sense, "fair": a "fine, plain, level state of equality, over which the beholder passed with pleasure"; a bright cloth or fabric spanning the entire country, a canopy of shelter and shared regard.[20]

We have so far shown how features that have been located at the site of the beautiful object (features such as the object's symmetry, equality, and pressure against lateral disregard) assist us in getting to justice. There remain two other sites—the "live" mental action of perceiving and the "live" action of creation—where the complicity between beauty and justice can again be seen.

But it will be helpful to locate ourselves and see what has so far been said. The equality of beauty enters the world before justice and stays longer because it does not depend on human beings to bring it about: though human beings have created much of the beauty of the world, they are only collaborators in a much vaster project. The world accepts our contributions but in no way depends on us. Even when beauty and justice are both in the world, beauty performs a special service because it is available to sensory perception in a way that justice (except in rare places like an assembly) normally is not, even though it is equally material and comes into being because of the fragility of the material world. By now we can begin to see that the equality of beauty, its pressure toward distribution, resides not just in its interior feature of symmetry but in its generously being present, widely present, to almost all people at almost all times—as in the mates that they choose to love, their children, the birds that fly through their garden, the songs they sing—a distributional availability that comes from its being external, present ("prae-sens"), standing before the senses.

When aesthetic fairness and ethical fairness are both present to perception, their shared commitment to equality can be seen as merely an analogy, for it may truly be said that when both terms of an analogy are present, the analogy is inert. It asks nothing more of us than that we occasionally notice it. But when one term ceases to be visible (either because it is not present, or because it is present but dispersed beyond our sensory field), then the analogy ceases to be inert: the term that is present becomes pressing, active, insistent, calling out for, directing our attention toward, what is absent. I describe this, focusing on touch, as a weight or lever, but ancient and medieval philosophers always referred to it acoustically: beauty is a call.

Radical Decentering

We have seen how the beautiful object—in its symmetry and generous sensory availability—assists in turning us to justice. The two other sites, that of the perceiver and that of the act of creation, also reveal the pressure beauty exerts toward ethical equality.

Once we move to these two sites, we enter into the live actions of perceiving and creating, and are therefore carried to the subject of aliveness, our final goal.

The surfaces of the world are aesthetically uneven. You come around a bend in the road, and the world suddenly falls open; you continue on around another bend, and go back to your conversation, until you are once more interrupted by the high bank of radiant meadow grass rising steeply beside the road. The same happens when you move through a sea of faces at the railroad station or rush down the aisle of a crowded lecture hall. Or you may be sweeping the garden bricks at home, attending with full scrutiny to each square inch of their mauve-orange-blue surfaces (for how else can you sweep them clean?); then suddenly a tiny mauve-orange-blue triangle, with a silver sheen, lifts off from the sand between the bricks where it had been sleepily camouflaged until the air currents disturbed it. It flutters in the air, then settles back down on the brick, demure, closed-winged, a triangle this big: △. Why should this tiny fragment of flying brick-color stop your heart?

Folded into the uneven aesthetic surfaces of the world is a pressure toward social equality. It comes from the object's symmetry, from the corrective pressure it exerts against lateral disregard, and from its own generous availability to sensory perception. But a reader may object that even if the idea of ethical fairness does come before one's mind at the moment one beholds something beautiful, the idea remains abstract. Nothing requires us to give up the ground that would begin to enact such symmetries. It is here that great assistance is provided by Simone Weil, whose mystical writings and life practices—working side by side with laborers in the Spanish Civil War; exacerbating the TB from which she was dying by refusing to eat more than her compatriots in France who were starving under German occupation—were inspired by her commitment to justice. (We are trying to hold steady to the agreement we made that we would, in this section, draw primarily from defenders of justice, not defenders of beauty, even though the two so often converge.)

At the moment we see something beautiful, we undergo a radical decentering. Beauty, according to Weil, requires us "to give up our imaginary position as the center. . . . A transformation then takes place at the very roots of our sensibility, in our immediate reception of sense impressions and psychological impressions."[21] Weil speaks matter-of-factly, often without illustration, implicitly requiring readers to test the truth of her assertion against their own experience. Her account is always deeply somatic: what happens, happens to our bodies. When we come upon beautiful things—the tiny mauve-orange-blue moth on the brick, Augustine's cake, a sentence about innocence in Hampshire—they act like small tears in the surface of the world that pull us through to some vaster space;[22] or they form "ladders reaching toward the beauty of the world,"[23] or they lift us (as though by the air currents of someone else's sweeping), letting the ground rotate beneath us several inches, so that when we land, we find we are standing in a different relation to the world than we were a moment before. It is not that we cease to stand at the center of the world, for we never stood there. It is that we cease to stand even at the center of our own world. We willingly cede our ground to the thing that stands before us.

The radical decentering we undergo in the presence of the beautiful is also described by Iris Murdoch in a 1967 lecture called "The Sovereignty of Good over Other Concepts." As this title indicates, her subject is goodness, not beauty. "Ethics," Murdoch writes, "should not be merely an analysis of ordinary mediocre conduct, it should be a hypothesis about good conduct and about how this can be achieved."[24] How we make choices, how we act, is deeply connected to states of consciousness, and so "anything which alters consciousness in the direction of unselfishness, objectivity and realism is to be connected with virtue." Murdoch then specifies the single best or most "obvious thing in our surroundings which is an occasion for 'unselfing' and that is what is popularly called beauty."[25]

She describes suddenly seeing a kestrel hovering: it brings about an "unselfing." It causes a cluster of feelings that normally promote the self (for she had been "anxious . . . resentful . . . brooding perhaps on some damage done to [her] prestige") now to fall away. It is not just that she becomes "self-forgetful" but that some more capacious mental act is possible: all the space formerly in the service of protecting, guarding, advancing the self (or its "prestige") is now free to be in the service of something else.

It is as though one has ceased to be the hero or heroine in one's own story and has become what in a folktale is called the "lateral figure" or "donor figure." It may sound not as though one's participation in a state of overall equality has been brought about, but as though one has just suffered a demotion. But at moments when we believe we are conducting ourselves with equality, we are usually instead conducting ourselves as the central figure in our own private story; and when we feel ourselves to be merely adjacent, or lateral (or even subordinate), we are probably more closely approaching a state of equality. In any event, it is precisely the ethical alchemy of beauty that what might in another context seem like a demotion is no longer recognizable as such: this is one of the cluster of feelings that have disappeared.

Radical decentering might also be called an opiated adjacency. A beautiful thing is not the only thing in the world that can make us feel adjacent; nor is it the only thing in the world that brings a state of acute pleasure. But it appears to be one of the few phenomena in the world that brings about both simultaneously: it permits us to be adjacent while also permitting us to experience extreme pleasure, thereby creating the sense that it is our own adjacency that is pleasure-bearing. This seems a gift in its own right, and a gift as a prelude to or precondition of enjoying fair relations with others. It is clear that an *ethical fairness* which requires "a symmetry of everyone's relation" will be greatly assisted by an *aesthetic fairness* that creates in all participants a state of delight in their own lateralness.

This lateral position continues in the third site of beauty, not now the suspended state of beholding but the active state of creating—the site of stewardship in which one acts to protect or perpetuate a fragment of beauty already in the world or instead to supplement it by bringing into being a new object. (The latter is more usually described as an act of creation than the former, but we have seen from the opening pages of this book forward that the two are prompted by the same impulse and should be perceived under a single rubric.) The way beauty at this third site presses us toward justice might seem hard to uncover since we know so little about "creation"; but it is not difficult to make a start since justice itself is dependent on human hands to bring it into being and has no existence independent of acts of creation. Beauty may be either natural or artifactual; justice is always artifactual and is therefore assisted by any perceptual event that so effortlessly incites in us the wish to create. Because beauty repeatedly brings us face-to-face with our own powers to create, we know where and how to locate those powers when a situation of injustice calls on us to create without itself guiding us, through pleasure, to our destination. The two distinguishable forms of creating beauty—perpetuating beauty that already exists; originating beauty that does not yet exist—have equivalents within the realm of justice, as one can hear in John Rawls's formulation of what, since the time of Socrates, has been known as the "duty to justice" argument: we have a duty, says Rawls, "to support" just arrangements where they already exist and to help bring them into being where they are "not yet established."

Another feature shared by the kind of creation we undertake on behalf of beauty and the kind of creation we undertake on behalf of justice has been suggested by political philosopher Andreas Eshete.[26]

In both realms, the object that one aspires to create may be completely known, partially known, or completely unknown to the creator. It is precisely on this basis that John Rawls differentiates three forms of justice: in "perfect justice" we know the outcome we aspire to achieve as well as the procedure by which that outcome can be brought about (food should be shared equally, and we can ensure this outcome by arranging that the person who slices the cake is also the last to select his own slice); in "imperfect justice" we know the outcome we aspire to achieve, and we know the procedure that gives us the best chance of approximating this outcome (persons guilty of a crime should be convicted and innocent persons should go free; a jury trial gives us the best hope of achieving this outcome, though it by no means guarantees it); in "pure procedural justice," finally, we have no picture of the best outcome, and we must trust wholly in the fairness of the procedures to ensure that the outcome itself is fair (here equality of opportunity is Rawls's illustration).[27] Aesthetic creation, too, has this same variation: one may have a vision of the object to be created and the path by which to bring it into being; one may instead have a vision of the object to be created and a technique that brings only its approximation into being; or one may have no prior vision and may simply entrust oneself to the action of creating (as in Richard

Wollheim's account of the way one learns what one has been drawing only when the drawing is done).[28]

The nonself-interestedness of the beholder has—to return to the subject of adjacency—been seen in a number of ways: first, in the absence of continuity between the beholder and the beheld (since the beholder does not become beautiful in the way that the pursuer of truth becomes knowledgeable); second, in the radical decenteredness the beholder undergoes in the presence of something or someone beautiful; third, in the willingness of the beholder to place himself or herself in the service of bringing new beauty into the world, creating a site of beauty separate from the self.

The unself-interestedness becomes visible in a fourth odd feature. Since beauty is pleasure-producing, one might assume that one would be avid to have it in one's own life and less avid, or noncommittal, about the part it should play in other people's lives. But is this the case? As was noticed at the opening, over the last several decades many people have either actively advocated a taboo on beauty or passively omitted it from their vocabulary, even when thinking and writing about beautiful objects such as paintings and poems. But if one asks them the following question—"Thinking not of ourselves but of people who will be alive at the end of the twenty-first century: is it your wish for them that they be beauty-loving?"—the answer seems to be "Yes"; and "Yes," delivered with speed and without hesitation. My own sample is informal and small, but does it not seem likely that a larger group would answer in similar fashion? If they would, the response suggests that whatever hardships we are willing to impose on ourselves we are not willing to impose on other people. Or perhaps phrased another way: however uncertain we are about whether the absence of beauty from our own lives is a benefit or a deficit, once we see the subject from a distant perspective, it instantly becomes clear that the absence of beauty is a profound form of deprivation.

A related outcome seems to occur if one asks people who are individually opposed to beauty to think in terms of our whole era or even century: "Do you hope that when people in the twenty-first and twenty-second centuries speak of us (the way we so effortlessly make descriptive statements about people living in the nineteenth or eighteenth or seventeenth centuries), do you hope these future people will describe us as beauty-loving? or instead as neutral with respect to beauty? or instead as beauty-disregarding?" Those I have questioned state their hope that we will be spoken about by future peoples as beauty-loving. Does it not seem reasonable to suppose that many people might give this same answer? Let us suppose this and then see what it would mean:

it would mean, oddly, that although beauty is highly particular and plural, one can suffer its loss to oneself, or even to those within the daily circle of one's activities, but cannot wish so grave a loss to the larger world of which one is a part, to the era in which one has lived. Neither from one's own century nor from any future century can one imagine its disappearance as anything but a deprivation.

There is one additional thought experiment that, like those above, seems to reinforce the recognition that beauty (though experienced intimately and acutely on each person's individual pulse) is unself-interested. Picture a population empowered to make decisions about the forms of beauty that will be present in our world and picture also that, in making decisions about this, none among them knew any of his or her own features: not gender, not geography, not talents or powers (level of sensory acuity, compositional abilities, physical agility, intellectual reach), not level of wealth, not intimacy or friendships. The population would make their judgments from behind "the veil of ignorance" that we now (at the invitation of John Rawls) often enlist in picturing decisions about social and economic arrangements but that may also assist us in clarifying our relation to the aesthetic surfaces of the world.

Suppose this population were presented with this question: "In the near future, human beings can arrange things so that there either will or will not be beautiful sky. Do you wish there to be beautiful sky?" (The issue before them is not the presence or absence of life-supporting oxygen for which wholly separate arrangements, due to technological advances, can swiftly be made; the question is about the way the sky's beauty itself is perceived to be part of a life-support system.) Because the sky is equally distributed throughout the world—because its beautiful events are equally distributed—it will not be surprising if the population in large numbers, or even unanimously, agree that the beautiful sky should continue. Because most of its manifestations—its habit of alternating between blue and black, the phases of the moon, the sunrise and sunset—are present everywhere, those voting do not need to know where they are living to know that they will be beneficiaries.

It is true that in addition to the constant sky events there are nonconstant ones, but these varied events are unvarying in the intensity of their beauty. The sky where I now am is subject to motions I have never known before, rivulets of air moving vertically up in streams that wash sideways, so that the black ravens and red-tailed hawks tumble in it all day, somersaulting and ferris-wheeling through the air, placing themselves in invisible fountains that lift them up until suddenly, tucking in their wings, they plunge rapidly down, spinning head over tail until out come their wings and the slow float upwards starts over again. But each piece of sky is like every other in being in some feature incomparable: one moves each day across five hundred shades of azure and aquamarine; another is so moist in its lavenders, silvers, and grays that the green ground beneath it glows and becomes a second sky; another on long winter nights becomes black with wide pulsing streams of pink, green, blue. The members of our population need not know the specific ground on which fate has placed them (Antigua, Ireland, Siberia) to know that they will be the beneficiaries of both shared and exceptional beauties of the sky. There is therefore no reason to construe their positive vote as anything other than self-interest.

The same outcome seems likely to occur if we ask this population their decision about blossoms. Although they are not so evenly distributed as the sky—in some latitudes covering the meadows for only six weeks and in other latitudes covering the hillsides almost year round—they are so generously distributed across the earth that it would not be surprising if people, without knowing anything about their own attributes, would affirm the continuous existence of plants and blossoms. The population might reason that whichever geography they find themselves living in (once they step out from behind the "veil of ignorance" and recover knowledge of their own features), their local ground will be better with, than without, flowers. So here again we have no reason to search for descriptions other than vibrant self-interest and self-survival, which are compatible with the intense somatic pleasure, the sentient immediacy of the experience of beauty.

But what if now the deliberation turned to objects and events that instead of being evenly distributed across the world were emphatically nondistributional. "Shall there be here and there an astonishingly beautiful underground cave whose passageways extend several miles, opening into crystal-lined grottos and large galleries of mineral latticework, in other galleries their mute walls painted by people who visited thousands of years earlier?" Those from whom we are seeking counsel cannot assume that they are likely to live near it, for they have been openly informed that the caves about which they are being asked to vote exist in only two places on earth. Nor can they even assume that if fate places them near one of the caves, they will be able to enter its deep interior, for climbing down into the galleries requires levels of physical agility and confidence beyond what are widely distributed among any population. But here is the question: isn't there every reason to suppose that the population will—even in the face of full knowledge that the cave is likely to be forever unavailable to them—request that such a cave be kept in existence, that it be protected and spared harm? Isn't it possible, even likely, that the population will respond in exactly the same way toward objects that are nondistributional as to those that are shared across the surface of the earth, that they will—as though they were thinking of skies and flowers—affirm the existence of remote caves and esoteric pieces of music (harder to enter even than the cave) and paintings that for many generations are held by private collectors and seen by almost no one's eyes?

People seem to wish there to be beauty even when their own self-interest is not served by it; or perhaps more accurately, people seem to intuit that their own self-interest is served by distant peoples' having the benefit of beauty. For although this was written as though it were a thought experiment, there is nothing speculative about it: the vote on blossoms has already been taken (people over many centuries have nurtured and carried the flowers from place to place, supplementing what was there); the vote on the sky has been taken (the recent environmental movement); and the vote on the caves has innumerable times been taken—otherwise it is inexplicable why people get so upset when they learn that a Vermeer painting has been stolen from the Gardner Museum without any assurance that its surface is being protected; why people get upset about the disappearance of kelp forests they had never even heard of until the moment they were informed of the loss; why museums, schools, universities take such care that beautiful artifacts from people long in the past be safely carried foward to people in the future. We are not guessing: the evidence is in.

NOTES

∽

THE NOTES that follow specify the English translation and edition used for works originally written in another language. Passages quoted from works originally written in English are not footnoted except where variations occur across different editions (as in the case of Emily Dickinson) or where the work may not be instantly familiar to the reader (as in the book form of Iris Murdoch's 1967 lecture).

PART ONE: ON BEAUTY AND BEING WRONG

1. The translation used here, and whenever Dante's *Vita nuova* is quoted, is Mark Musa (New York: Oxford University Press, 1992), xv, xvi, 29, 30.

2. Marcel Proust, *Remembrance of Things Past*, trans. C. K. Scott Moncrieff and Terence Kilmartin (New York: Vintage–Random House, 1982), 1:706–7.

3. Simone Weil, "Love of the Order of the World," in *Waiting for God*, trans. Emma Craufurd, introd. Leslie A. Fiedler (New York: Harper & Row, 1951), 180.

4. Emily Dickinson, *The Poems of Emily Dickinson: Variorum Edition*, ed. R. W. Franklin (Cambridge: Harvard University Press, Belknap Press, 1998), 785. Variants in wording in other editions are given on the same page. My thanks to Helen Vendler for bringing

to my attention this poem as well as "The Beginning of the End," the poem by Gerard Manley Hopkins I several times quote.

5. I am using Robert Fagles's translation of *The Odyssey*, introd. Bernard Knox (New York: Penguin, 1996), Bk. 6, 168–72, 175–86. Most lines cited are from Book 6; occasionally a phrase from Book 5 or 7 enters.

6. Augustine, *De Musica*, trans. W. F. Jackson Knight, in *Philosophies of Art and Beauty*, ed. Albert Hofstadter and Richard Kuhns (Chicago: University of Chicago Press, 1976), 196.

7. As Nausicaa greets Odysseus on the beach, so a short time later Athena greets him when he arrives at the city: "As he was about to enter the welcome city, the bright-eyed goddess herself came up to greet him there." The idea of beauty as a greeting reappears in many classical, medieval, and Renaissance writings— in the description of beauty's "clear discernibility" in Plato, in the attention to the attribute of *claritas* in Aquinas, in the account of beauty as "a call" in both Albertus Magnus and Ficino. In Dante's *Vita nuova* the idea of beauty as a greeting becomes not just a theme or argument but a principle of structure, for the work is organized as a succession of greetings. "It was precisely the ninth hour of that day (three o'clock in the afternoon), when her sweet greeting reached me," reports Dante of Beatrice; and his first sonnet begins: "To every loving heart and captive soul ... greetings I bring." A greeting, either given or withheld, is the central action and issue throughout. The idea continues across the centuries. When James Joyce's Lynch announces that he is devoted to beauty, Stephen Dedalus responds by lifting his cap in greeting.

8. The English words "energetic" and "melting" occur in various translations of the Sixteenth Letter of Schiller's *On the Aesthetic Education of Man in a Series of Letters*, such as that by Reginald Snell (New York: Frederick Ungar, 1954) and again that by Elizabeth M. Wilkinson and L. A. Willoughby (Oxford: Clarendon, 1967).

9. Shakespeare's sonnets (and a small number of other beautiful things) openly promise that they will be forever beautiful; but most beautiful things make no such claim. They only seem to make such a claim because the very moment they enter our minds, there simultaneously enters our minds a wish that this thing should forever be what it is now. So associated are the two events that the object itself seems to have made the announcement that it will always be what it is now.

10. Physicist Thomas Appelquist, for example, has told me that in particle physics the beauty of a theory is taken to be predictive of its truth; experimental astrophysicist Paul Horowitz, on the other hand, counsels new physicists not to assume that if they come up with a "pretty" theory, it must be true. Exponents of both positions can no doubt be found within each of the two sciences.

PART TWO: ON BEAUTY AND BEING FAIR

1. Indeed, at the very moment when beauty was being banished from universities for distracting from social justice, scholars trying to make problems of social justice visible were sometimes accused of "reenacting" the cruelty by making suffering available to the reader's gaze.

2. Ps. 90:17 (King James Version).

3. So odd does such a prohibition sound that it may appear I am inventing the idea for the sake of the argument; yet over the last fifteen years, many students, even the brightest and most good-hearted among them, have (as a result of the general prohibition on beauty) spoken in their papers about the way a poet or novelist reifies a garden or a flower or a beautiful bird by his or her lavish regard.

4. I do not know whether it is possible for a worshiper to have mental pictures of Jesus or Artemis or Krishna or Buddha or

Sarasvati, while withholding from mental view their beauty, but for the duration of the one sentence above, I will assume for the sake of argument that this is possible.

5. It might be objected that even the gardener, in trying to heighten the beauty of a particular bed, might tear out a plant, therefore harming its life; for the gardener, like Keats's poet, carries out "innumerable compositions and decompositions" to arrive at "the snail-horn perception of Beauty." But at most this means that gardeners should be prohibited from tearing out any already existing plant, which should stay where it is or be transplanted to a safe location (a rule some gardeners follow).

But what about the case where the gardener, seeking to make the garden more beautiful, *does* roughly dispose of the plant? Should we conclude that beauty imperils, rather than intensifies, the life contract? One way of answering the question is to ask whether the human protection accorded plants is higher or lower in the garden than in the world outside the garden. When we make this comparison we see that although the gardener has only imperfectly protected the plants, he has given them far more protection than they ordinarily receive. Another approach is to compare the flower garden, where the plants are grown for their beauty, with a vegetable garden, where the plants are grown for the gardener's table. The gardener in the flower garden places himself or herself in voluntary servitude to the flowers; the gardener in the vegetable garden has subordinated the life of the plant to the dinner table. I am not here objecting to the human need to eat; I am simply making the obvious point that in general "beauty" is associated with a life compact or contract, where the perceiver abstains from harming, or even actively enters into the protection of, this fragment of the world.

6. Immanuel Kant, *Observations on the Feeling of the Beautiful and Sublime*, trans. John T. Goldthwait, (Berkeley and Los Angeles:

University of California Press, 1960). The terms listed here occur on 46–49 (passim), 60, 78, 93, 97.

7. The sublime is sometimes credited with having multiplied the kinds of objects that could thereafter be perceived as "aesthetic." But most of the objects in both categories had formerly occupied a territory held under the inclusive rubric of beauty. Plato's or Aquinas's or Dante's conception of beauty had not been limited to the "good-hearted and cheerful." More important, the slightly scornful ring of "the good-hearted and cheerful" in that previous sentence only becomes possible once those adjectives have been severed from their aesthetic siblings, as the laughing angels on the edifice of Rheims Cathedral make clear.

8. Ernest Klein, *A Comprehensive Etymological Dictionary of the English Language* (Amsterdam: Elsevier Publishing, 1971), s.v. "welcome."

9. The conclusions reached about the etymology of "fair" in C. T. Onions's *Oxford Dictionary of English Etymology* (Oxford: Oxford Clarendon, 1966), Klein's *Comprehensive Etymological Dictionary*, and Eric Partridge's *Origins: A Short Etymological Dictionary of Modern English* (New York: Macmillan, 1966) are all in accord with one another, though it is only Klein who directly links the word "fair" to the word for "pact" by focusing on the verb "fay."

10. Because this event happened in childhood, the exact book Amartya Sen was reading has receded from view. Aristotelian philosopher Alan Code suggests several possibilities. In the discussion of distributive justice in *Nicomachean Ethics*, Book 5, chapter 3, Aristotle writes that equality has two terms but justice has four terms; a particular translation of, or commentary upon, this passage may have introduced the figure of the cube, especially since Aristotle observes, "This kind of proportion is termed by mathematicians geometrical proportion" (trans. H. Rackham, in Loeb edition, *Aristotle*, vol. 19 [Cambridge: Harvard University Press, 1934]).

Benjamin Jowett in his introductions to both Book 6 and Book 9 of Plato's *Republic* alludes to the contemporary belief that justice was a cube, and Plato's own statements in section 546a–547a, discussing cubes, perfect numbers, and the nuptial number of "divine beginnings," may be consistent with such a belief.

11. Throughout the 1990s, articles appeared in key science journals such as *Nature* claiming (1) that "symmetry" is by birds, butterflies, and other creatures chosen in mating over every other feature (such as size, color), possibly because it is taken as a visible manifestation of overall sturdiness of the genetic material; (2) that infants in different cultures stare longer at faces that are highly symmetrical, and also prefer classical music whose passages are symmetrically arranged over the same classical pieces whose musical phrases have been randomly reordered; and (3) that adults choose faces with symmetrical features (nose and mouth precisely equidistant between eyes), and seem to make identical choices across such distant cultures as Scotland and Japan. The research in all three areas is controversial and may well be overturned or qualified over the next decade. But even if the extreme claims of this research are retracted, symmetry will without doubt remain an important element in assessments of beauty.

12. This is again the W. F. Jackson Knight translation of *De Musica*, 186, 190, 191, 194, 201. Augustine perceives "equality" not just in a formal feature such as symmetry but in color: a patch of blue (or green or red or yellow) continually iterates itself across the surface it occupies.

13. The importance of a doctrinal location is visible in the debates about conscientous objection. See, for example, the special issue of *Rutgers Law Review* 21, no. 7 (Fall 1966) on "Civil Disobedience and the Law."

14. Bruce Russett, *Grasping the Democratic Peace: Principles for a Post-Cold War World* (Princeton: Princeton University Press, 1993), 59.

15. J. S. Morrison and J. F. Coates, *The Athenian Trireme: The History and Reconstruction of an Ancient Greek Warship* (Cambridge: Cambridge University Press, 1986). See also Lionel Casson, *Ships and Seamanship in the Ancient World* (Princeton: Princeton University Press, 1971).

16. "Concerning the Poet," in *Where Silence Reigns: Selected Prose by Rainer Maria Rilke*, trans. G. Craig Houston, foreword by Denise Levertov (New York: New Directions, 1978), 65–66.

17. Mary Ryan, "The American Parade: Representations of the Nineteenth-Century Social Order," in *The New Cultural History*, ed. Lynn Hunt (Berkeley and Los Angeles: University of California Press, 1989), 131–53.

18. Rowing as a vehicle of democracy in the United States is argued by Helen A. Cooper in *Thomas Eakins: The Rowing Pictures* (New Haven: Yale University Press and Yale Art Gallery, 1996), 24–25, 36, 44.

19. Eakins expresses his vision of the painter as rower in a March 6, 1868, letter to his father cited in ibid., 32.

20. Cassius, *Considerations on the Society or Order of Cincinnati, Lately Instituted by the Major-Generals, Brigadiers, and Other Officers of the American Army, Proving that it Creates, A Race of Hereditary Patricians, or Nobility, and Interspersed with Remarks on its Consequences to the Freedom and Happiness in the Republick*, reprinted in *Anglo-American Antimilitary Tracts 1697–1830*, ed. R. Kohn (New York: Arno Press, 1979). The beautiful fabric or canopy of military equality is spoken of by secretary of war General Knox in his 1786 proposal to Congress for a militia, quoted in the 1863 tract by J. Willard, *Plan for the General Arrangement of the Militia of the United States* (Boston: J. Wilson & Sons), 29; and again by William Sumner in 1826, *A Paper on the Militia Presented to the Hon. James Barbour, Secretary of War* (Washington: B. Homans, 1833), 9. See also Ransom Gillet's address to the House of Representatives, *Congressional Globe*, 24th Cong., 1st sess., 1836, 235, 237.

21. Weil, "Love of the Order of the World," in *Waiting for God,* 159.

22. Ibid., 163.

23. Ibid., 180.

24. Iris Murdoch, *The Sovereignty of Good over Other Concepts: The Leslie Stephen Lecture* (Cambridge: Cambridge University Press, 1967), 2.

25. Ibid., 10.

26. Andreas Eshete, conversation with author, January 1998.

27. John Rawls, *A Theory of Justice* (Cambridge: Harvard University Press, 1971), 83–87. Other references throughout Part Two to John Rawls's ideas about fairness can be found on 12, 115.

28. Richard Wollheim, "On Drawing an Object," in *On Art and Mind* (Cambridge: Harvard University Press, 1974), 3–30.

ACKNOWLEDGMENTS

I am deeply grateful to Yale University for inviting me to give the Tanner Lectures in 1998, to the Tanner Foundation for wishing to bring new lectures (as well as new fountains) into the world, to the Getty Research Institute for the sunlit time and silver olive trees under which the writing was completed, and to many beauty-loving students, colleagues, and friends (your breath is in this book).

Four times during the 1990s I had the chance to teach a graduate seminar on beauty, three times at Harvard University and once at the School of Criticism and Theory. The subject matter drew to my door ardent students from the humanities and (less often, but not less ardent) from math, physics, astrophysics, biochemistry. My thanks to them, and to my research assistant Nick Davis, who during both the preparation of the lectures and the preparation of the book provided help that was swift, precise, inventive.

I have a special thanks to those who guided the manuscript through its final hours. The suggestions made by senior manuscript editor Lauren Lepow were always right. D. A. Miller, Ayana Haviv, Emory Elliott, and Michael Roth were among the book's first readers and brought it to life.

Should this small object make a safe passage through the world, it will be the work of Mary Murrell at Princeton University Press, whose vision has steadily outpaced mine and whose delicate hand has touched every page.